ONE

ONE

Essential Writings on Nonduality

EDITED BY JERRY KATZ

SENTIENT PUBLICATIONS, LLC

First Sentient Publications edition 2007

For permissions, see page 199.

A paperback original

Cover design by Kim Johansen, Black Dog Design
Book design by Nicholas Cummings

Library of Congress Cataloging-in-Publication Data

Katz, Jerry, 1949-
One : essential writings on nonduality / by Jerry Katz.
p. cm.
ISBN-13: 978-1-59181-053-7
1. Spiritual life. 2. Self-realization—Religious aspects. 3. Ramana, Maharshi. I. Title.

BL624.K35 2006
111'.82—dc22

2006028151

Printed in the United States of America

10 9 8 7 6 5 4

SENTIENT PUBLICATIONS
A Limited Liability Company
1113 Spruce St.
Boulder, CO 80302
www.sentientpublications.com

To everyone I ever met on the Internet

Contents

Part One: What Is Nonduality? 1

Desire and the "Path" 6

Part Two: Bhagavan Sri Ramana Maharshi 9

The Essential Teachings 15

On Practice 31

Part Three: Nondual Confessions 39

Advaita Vedanta 42

Sufism 42

Judaism 43

Taoism 43

Native American Tradition 44

Christianity 44

Buddhism 45

Relating to These Writings and to Self-Realized People 45

Our Real Job 46

Advaita Vedanta: The Avadhuta Gita 47

Introduction by Swami Ashokananda 47

The Avadhuta Gita (verses 1 – 41) 48

Sufism: The One Alone 55

Introduction by Shaykh Tosun Bayrak al-Jerrahi al-Halveti 55

The One Alone 57

Judaism: The Essential Kabbalah 63

Nonduality 63

God's Encampment 64

The Chain of Being 64

Ein Sof and You 65

You Enliven Everything 65

Ein Sof 65

The Aroma of Infinity 66
Oblivion 67
Ayin 67
The Name of Nothingness 67
Being and Nothingness 68
Think of Yourself as Ayin 68
The Annihilation of Thought 68

TAOISM: *The Tao Te Ching* 69
Introduction by Victor H. Mair 69
Selections from the Tao Te Ching 71

NATIVE AMERICAN TRADITION: THE WAYS OF THE SPIRIT 77
Introduction by Kent Nerburn 77
The Ways of the Spirit 81

CHRISTIANITY: STEPS IN MY CHRISTIAN PASSAGE 89
Ascension 92
Incarnation 94
In the End 98

BUDDHISM: THE DIAMOND SUTRA 101
Introduction by A. F. Price 101
The Diamond Sutra 102
Because It Is Not, by Wei Wu Wei 108

Part Four: Nondual Perspectives 113

PSYCHOTHERAPY: THE SACRED MIRROR 121

EDUCATION: CHANGING THE HEART OF EDUCATION 131
Nothing: What You've Been Looking For 132
Don't Trust Anyone over Three 135
The Profound Knowledge of Not Knowing 137
Spirituality and Learning 140

ART: AN ARTIST'S JOURNEY OF TRANSFORMATION 143
I Became Nothing 143
The Stalemate with Formlessness 145

Willing Participants in the Unfolding 149
The Inspired Heart 151
A Return to the New 154
Doing Our Own Work First 156

Cinema: Journey to the Source—Decoding *The Matrix Trilogy* 159
The Plot of *The Matrix* 160
The Matrix World 163

Part Five: Conclusion 175

The Radical Nature of Nonduality 179

The Heart Sutra and the Nature of Nonduality 181

Things Stand Out Shining 187

The Worthwhile and the Impossible 189

Notes 191

Acknowledgments 197

Permissions 199

Index 201

No words can directly convey the truth that there is only nonduality.

—John Levy

Part One

What Is Nonduality?

NONDUALITY IS THE EXPERIENCE OF OUR TRUE NATURE, THE TASTE OF being. But when we try to describe what this true nature is, the written word often falls short. No one would mistake their knowledge of what a tree is for an actual tree, but in the realm of consciousness and spirituality, people sometimes feel that if they "know" what their true nature is, they've got it. However, being, by its very nature, can't be known, so words can only give us the direction in which to look.

The desire for spiritual growth is like every other desire. It may lead to mystical experience, to inner peace and greater wisdom. Perhaps we become comfortable in ashrams, around gurus, and at gatherings and retreats. Meditation, yoga, and spirituality fill our lives. For a while our desire feels satisfied. But after months or years, the desire returns. Now we learn that our desire for mystical experience, spiritual wisdom, or inner peace was the wish for another thing to possess.

We remain unsatisfied. Our spiritual need is now directed toward something unlike any spiritual experience or knowledge we have ever imagined. This "something" lies beyond experience and growth, beyond knowledge, beyond possession. We intuit that the fulfillment of this desire is the end to stress, anxiety, desperation, and fear, and the opening to freedom, joy, and simplicity.

This something could be called truth. When the thirst for truth is met, the sense of being separate from truth is gone. Nonduality literally means *not two*, which describes our relationship to truth. We, and our desires, do not disappear in truth; they simply become seen as not separate.

The nature of truth is *not two*. If truth were separate from us, it would be a truth of duality. Far from providing relief from stress and fear, a life of duality would be a life of unfulfilled desires. We know that kind of "truth." It is our common world in which one thing after another promises to satisfy us, including spiritual things.

In childhood culture we were handed a clue about how to manage our urge for that something:

Tin Woodsman: What have you learned, Dorothy?

Dorothy: Well, I—I think that it—it wasn't enough to just want to see Uncle Henry and Auntie Em—and it's that—if I ever go looking for my heart's desire again, I won't look any further than my own backyard. Because if it isn't there, I never really lost it to begin with! Is that right?

Glinda: That's all it is.[1]

Our heart's desire and who, what, and where we are, are not separate.

Our pursuit for truth is for the full recognition of non-separation, not-two-ness, or nonduality. The value of this quality of desire is confirmed in the first verse of the scripture from Hindu tradition known as the *Avadhuta Gita,* or *Song of the Free*:

> Through the grace of God alone, the desire for nonduality arises in wise people to save them from great fear.[2]

The need for knowing nonduality, or non-separation from truth, is grace, a profound gift arising from truth. The desire, the *Avadhuta Gita* says, arises in wise people. We could say the hunger for nonduality is wisdom. Wisdom is allowing the desire for nonduality to unfold. That is the way to be saved from fear.

We've talked about two kinds of desire: common desire, including the desire for spiritual experience and growth, and the desire for nonduality. We may also speak of two kinds of fear. The everyday kind is fear of loss: loss of friends, lovers, money, jobs, power, possessions, health, our personal status quo, and life. As with common desires, the easing of one fear makes room for the arising of another. Everyday fear and its associated mental conditions of despair, anxiety, and grief, continue.

The second kind of fear is what the *Avadhuta Gita* calls "great fear," and there are two kinds of great fear. One is the fear that we do not exist, that we are not. Charlotte Joko Beck wrote: "Intelligent practice always deals with just one thing: the fear at the base of human existence, the fear that I am not. And of course I am not, but the last thing I want to know is that."[3]

What saves us from "great fear"—and all fear—is the *desire* for nonduality. That is, what saves us from the fear of nonduality is the desire for nonduality, a simple statement that could be applied to any fear.

We have already noted that we may feel the opposite, that common life is not real, that we remain unsatisfied with all our spiritual endeavors, and that the sense of "I am not" is what is real. The second great fear is that we are missing what is real, what is true. The desire for nonduality saves us from that fear.

According to the *Avadhuta Gita*, by God's grace the desire for nonduality—for the full recognition that we are not—arises within us. If our wish is for experiences, knowledge, awareness of subtle things, or anything other than the recognition that we are not—then our desire is no different than the desires for ice cream, a diploma, a spouse, a vacation: all good things, but they may lead to further wants.

The desire for truth or nonduality, if it is not avoided, sets us forth in a new direction.

DESIRE AND THE "PATH"

Eugen Herrigel, in his book *Zen in the Art of Archery*, describes the passion for nonduality:

> Why I took up Zen, and for this purpose set out to learn the art of archery, needs some explanation. Even as a student I had, as though driven by a secret urge, been preoccupied with mysticism, despite the mood of the times, which had little use for such interests...Nowhere did I find anything approaching satisfactory answers to my questions...I found myself confronted by locked doors, and yet I could not refrain from constantly rattling at the handles. But the longing persisted, and, when it grew weary, the longing for this longing.[4]

Elsewhere in the book Herrigel states:

> If he is irresistibly driven towards this goal, he must set out on his way again, take the road to the artless art. He must dare to leap into the Origin, so as to live by the Truth and in the Truth, like one who has become one with it.[5]

We, too, move forth "driven by a secret urge." Desire fuels the unfolding of our lives, but truth, or nondual reality, is not separate from us. There is no going from non-truth to truth, from Oz to our own backyard. When our desire for nonduality is resolved, *there* is the recognition of truth or the nondual nature of reality. That recognition is not extraordinary, even if the life prior to that recognition was fantastic. Using "eternity consciousness" for truth, John Wren-Lewis wrote:

> Perhaps the most extraordinary feature of eternity consciousness is that it doesn't feel extraordinary at all. It feels

> quintessentially natural that personal consciousness should be aware of its own Ground, while my first fifty-nine years of so-called "normal" consciousness, in ignorance of that Ground, now seem like a kind of waking dream. It was as if I'd been entranced from birth into a collective nightmare of separate individuals struggling in an alien universe for survival, satisfaction and significance.[6]

The pursuit of nonduality, when resolved, is recognition of something fundamentally not separate from our own backyard.

But the sense may remain that we are on a journey, and we want to know where to focus our attention to serve our desire. We shall begin by considering the teachings and instruction of Bhagavan Sri Ramana Maharshi, perhaps the most famous nondualist of the twentieth century. Ramana Maharshi's instruction includes two injunctions: to attend to the I-thought so that we may know its source, and to surrender to Self, God, truth, or nondual reality. Although these practices are mentioned throughout the book, at times offhandedly, I would like to impress that to follow the instructions for inquiry and surrender is for most people a difficult, seemingly impossible task. Even though we may be urged on by the fear that we are missing what is true, we may at some point become frozen by the fear that we "are not," that we do not exist. Even if we think we want to know the state of "I am not," great fear strikes when we realize we cannot know such a state, and there cannot *be* such a state.

Great fears aside, those inclined will begin the practices discussed in the next two chapters. Progress achieved in these practices will probably benefit anyone's life. We will come to view life from the perspective of "being" rather than "being this" or "being that." That perspective gives peace, provides some relief to suffering.

Therefore, if at this time in our lives we do not fully understand the extreme teaching of nonduality, which reveals itself in statements such as "there cannot be such a state," or "we do not exist," we can still get some good out of what we read and learn here. That is to say, both the impossible and the worthwhile are contained in this book.

Part Two

Bhagavan Sri Ramana Maharshi

Sri Ramana Maharshi does not use the term *nonduality*. Instead he speaks of the Self, the Heart, God, which all mean nondual reality or truth. David Godman writes in *Be as You Are: The Teachings of Sri Ramana Maharshi*:

> The Self … is the term that [Ramana Maharshi] used the most frequently. He defined it by saying that the real Self or real "I" is, contrary to perceptible experience, not an experience of individuality but a non-personal, all-inclusive awareness. It is not to be confused with the individual self which he said was essentially non-existent, being a fabrication of the mind which obscures the true experience of the real Self. He maintained that the real Self is always present and always experienced but he emphasized that one is only consciously aware of it as it really is when the self-limiting tendencies of the mind have ceased. Permanent and continuous Self-awareness is known as Self-realization.[1]

According to Ramana Maharshi, "the very fact that you are possessed of the quest of the Self is a manifestation of the divine grace."[2] "That which constitutes offering [oneself] up to the Self is living the life that shines, free of the false delusive mind."

"Peace is your natural state. It is the mind that obstructs the natural state," he says. The mind, therefore, is the source of fear. "Bondage is delusion of mind, a false sensation." "The ego alone is bondage, and one's own true nature, free of the contagion of the ego, is liberation." The desire for nonduality, which is given by grace, frees us from the bondage of the mind or the ego, which is the source of all fear, small and great. Ramana Maharshi further states, "The individual soul, having the form of 'I', is the ego. The Self, which is of the nature of consciousness, has no sense of 'I'." Hence no fear.

Ramana Maharshi plainly states: "There is no reaching the Self. If Self were to be reached, it would mean that the Self is not here and now but that it is yet to be obtained. … the Self is not reached. You are the Self; you are already That." This is the definition of nonduality: no separation from Self or truth.

Before we take a look at Ramana Maharshi's teachings, here is an introduction to the man himself:

> Bhagavan Sri Ramana Maharshi (1879 - 1950) was probably the most famous Indian sage of the twentieth century. He was renowned for his saintly life, for the fullness of his self-realization, and for the feelings of deep peace that visitors experienced in his presence. So many people came to see him at the holy hill of Arunachala where he spent his adult life that an ashram had to be built around him. He answered questions for hours every day, but never considered himself to be anyone's guru.
>
> He was born of middle-class parents on December 30, 1879, in a village called Tirucculi about 30 miles south of Madurai in southern India, and was named Venkataraman. His father died when Venkataraman was twelve, and so the boy went to live with his uncle in Madurai, where he

attended American Mission High School.

At age 16, he became spontaneously self-realized. Six weeks later the teen-aged boy ran away to the holy hill of Arunachala where he would remain for the rest of his life. For several years he stopped talking and spent many hours each day in samadhi (a trance-like absorption in the Self). When he began speaking again, people came to ask questions, and he soon acquired a reputation as a sage. In 1907, when Venkataraman was 28, an early devotee named him Bhagavan Sri Ramana Maharshi, Divine Eminent Ramana the Great Seer, and the name stuck. Ramana Maharshi died of cancer in 1950 at the age of 70.[3]

The Essential Teachings

Bhagavan Sri Ramana Maharshi

THIS CHAPTER DESCRIBES THE PRACTICES THAT ALLOW US TO CARRY through our desire for nonduality: inquiry, or attention to I-thought so that we may know its source, and surrender to Self or God.

We are reminded that we are not separate from the Self. Because we are not separate from the Self, the Self cannot be reached as though it is at Point B while we are at Point A. But the Self can be realized or recognized. Sri Ramana Maharshi talks about the nature of Self, the nature of mind and ego, and where and how to turn our attention. The material in this and the following chapter was selected by David Godman from published works of Ramana Maharshi.

Question: How can I attain Self-realization?

Bhagavan: Realization is nothing to be gained afresh; it is already there. All that is necessary is to get rid of the thought, "I have not realized."

Stillness or peace is realization. There is no moment when the Self is not. So long as there is doubt or the feeling of non-realization, the attempt should be made to rid oneself of these thoughts. They are due to the identification of the Self with the not-Self. When the not-Self disappears, the Self alone remains. To make room, it is enough that the cramping be removed; room is not brought in from elsewhere.

Question: Since realization is not possible without vasana-kshya [destruction of mental habits and tendencies], how am I to realize that state in which the vasanas [mental tendencies] are effectively destroyed?

Bhagavan: You are in that state now!

Question: Does it mean that by holding on to the Self, the vasanas should be destroyed as and when they emerge?

Bhagavan: They will themselves be destroyed if you remain as you are.

Question: How shall I reach the Self?

Bhagavan: There is no reaching the Self. If Self were to be reached, it would mean that the Self is not here and now but that it is yet to be obtained. What is got afresh will also be lost. So it will be impermanent. What is not permanent is not worth striving for. So I say the Self is not reached. You *are* the Self; you are already That.

The fact is, you are ignorant of your blissful state.

Ignorance supervenes and draws a veil over the pure Self which is bliss. Attempts are directed only to remove this veil of ignorance, which is merely wrong knowledge. The wrong knowledge is the false identification of the Self with the body, mind, etc. This false identification must go, and then the Self alone remains.

Therefore, realization is for everyone. Realization makes no difference between the aspirants. This very doubt, whether you can realize, and the notion 'I-have-not-realized' are themselves the obstacles. Be free from these obstacles also.[1]

In the experience of one's own true state of knowledge, one's real nature, the ideas of bondage and liberation do not exist. There is no attainment of liberation from bondage in the ultimate state of supreme truth, except in one's imagination.

It is because the mind, the vain ego, is habituated to the thought of bondage that enthusiastic efforts to attain liberation arise. Separation and union exist only through the ignorance of the jiva [the individual self]. They do not exist in the nature of the real, which is jnana [true knowledge] only.[2]

Question: What is true knowledge?

Bhagavan: It is that state of stillness, pure consciousness, which is experienced by the aspirant and which is like the waveless ocean or the motionless ether.[3]

Question: What is the state of attainment of knowledge?

Bhagavan: It is firm and effortless abidance in the Self in which the mind which has become one with the Self does not subsequently emerge again at any time. Each person, when he thinks of his body, usually and naturally has the idea, "I am not a goat or a cow, or any other animal, but a human being." Similarly, when he naturally has the Self-awareness, "I am not the fundamental physical entities, beginning with the body ... but the Self which is existence-consciousness-bliss," this is said to be the attainment of firm knowledge.[4]

Question: Is there any authority for saying that there is neither bondage nor liberation?

Bhagavan: This is decided on the strength of experience and not merely on the strength of the scriptures.

Question: If it is experienced, how is it experienced?

Bhagavan: "Bondage" and "Liberation" are mere linguistic terms. They have no reality of their own. Therefore, they cannot function of their own accord. It is necessary to accept the existence of some basic thing of which they are the modifications. If one enquires, "For whom is there bondage and liberation?" it will be seen, "They are for me." If one enquires, "Who am I?", one will see that there is no such thing as the "I." It will then be as clear as an amalaka fruit in one's hand that what remains is one's real being. As this truth will be naturally and clearly experienced by those who leave aside mere verbal discussions and enquire into themselves inwardly, at least for a moment, there is no doubt that all realized persons uniformly see neither bondage nor liberation so far as the true Self is concerned.

Question: If truly there is neither bondage nor liberation, what is the reason for the actual experience of sorrow and delusion?

Bhagavan: They appear to be real only when one swerves from

one's real nature. They will never appear in the natural state.

Question: Is it possible for everyone to know directly without doubt what exactly is one's true nature?

Bhagavan: There is no need at all to doubt that it is possible.[5]

If you enquire into the Self and come to know it, in that vision of the Self the age-old primal illusion of bondage will become a story long-forgotten. In the hearts of those who have investigated and come to know reality as it actually is, liberation in all its clarity is eternally attained.

What is always natural to everyone is liberation, which is bliss. Bondage is delusion of mind, a false sensation. The ego alone is bondage, and one's own true nature, free of the contagion of the ego, is liberation.

There is no greater deception than [believing that] liberation, which is ever present as one's own nature, will be attained at some later stage. Even the desire for liberation is the work of delusion. Therefore, remain still.[6]

The individual soul, having the form of "I," is the ego. The Self, which is of the nature of consciousness, has no sense of "I." Nor does the insentient body possess a sense of "I." The intermediate appearance of a delusive ego between consciousness and the inert body is the root cause of all the troubles. Upon its destruction, by whatever means, that which really exists will shine as it really is. This is called liberation.[7]

Those who are established in this state never swerve from their true state. The terms "silence" [mauna] and "remaining still" [summa iruttal] refer to this state alone.[8]

Question: Is the state of "being still" a state involving effort or effortlessness?

Bhagavan: It is not an effortless state of indolence. All mundane activities which are ordinarily called effort are performed with the aid of a portion of the mind and with frequent breaks. But the act of communion with the Self, or remaining still inwardly, is perfect effort, which is performed with the entire mind and without break.

Maya [delusion or ignorance] which cannot be destroyed by any other act is completely destroyed by this perfect effort, which is called "silence" [mauna].[9]

Question: How can I control the mind?

Bhagavan: There is no mind to control if the Self is realized. The Self shines forth when the mind vanishes. In the realized man the mind may be active or inactive, [but for him] the Self alone exists. For, the mind, body and world are not separate from the Self; and they cannot remain apart from the Self. Can they be other than the Self? When aware of the Self why should one worry about these shadows? How do they affect the Self?

Question: If the mind is merely a shadow, how then is one to know the Self?

Bhagavan: The Self is the Heart, self-luminous. Illumination arises from the Heart and reaches the brain, which is the seat of the mind. The world is seen with the mind; so you see the world by the reflected light of the Self. The world is perceived by an act of the mind. When the mind is illumined it is aware of the world; when it is not so illumined, it is not aware of the world.

If the mind is turned in, towards the source of illumination, objective knowledge ceases, and the Self alone shines as the Heart.

The moon shines by reflecting the light of the sun. When the sun has set, the moon is useful for displaying objects. When the sun has risen, no one needs the moon, though its disc is visible in the sky. So it is with the mind and the Heart. The mind is made useful by its reflected light. It is used for seeing objects. When turned inwards, it merges into the source of illumination which shines by itself, and the mind is then like the moon in the daytime.

When it is dark, a lamp is necessary to give light. But when the sun has arisen, there is no need for the lamp; the objects are visible. And to see the sun no lamp is necessary; it is enough if you turn your eyes towards the self-luminous sun. Similarly with the mind; to see objects the light reflected from the mind is necessary. To see the Heart it is enough that the mind is turned towards it. Then the mind does not count and the Heart is self-effulgent.[10]

Question: How does individuality emanate from the Absolute Self, and how is its return made possible?

Bhagavan: As a spark proceeds from fire, individuality emanates from the Absolute Self. The spark is called the ego. In the case of the ajnani [the unenlightened person], the ego identifies itself with some object simultaneously with its rise. It cannot remain without such association with objects.

This association is due to ajnana [ignorance], whose destruction is the objective of one's efforts. If this tendency to identify itself with objects is destroyed, the ego becomes pure and then it also merges into its source. The false identification of oneself with the body is dehatmabuddhi or "I-am-the-body" idea. This must go before good results can follow.[11]

Question: How can any inquiry initiated by the ego reveal its own unreality?

Bhagavan: The ego's phenomenal existence is transcended when you dive into the source wherefrom arises the aham-vritti [the thought of "I," the sense of being an individual person].

Self-inquiry by following the clue of aham-vritti is just like the dog tracing its master by his scent. The master may be at some distant, unknown place, but that does not at all stand in the way of the dog tracing him. The master's scent is an infallible clue for the animal, and nothing else, such as the dress he wears, or his build and stature, etc., counts. The dog holds on to that scent undistractedly while searching for him, and finally it succeeds in tracing him.[12]

The unique ray that shines within the jiva [individual self] as "I" exists as the clue. If the jiva unflaggingly traces the source of that ray to the Heart, it will discover the Supreme and its bondage will cease.[13]

Question: The question still remains why the quest for the source of aham-vritti [the "I"-thought], as distinguished from other vrittis [mental activities or modifications], should be considered the direct means to Self-realization.

Bhagavan: Although the concept of "I"-ness or "I-am"-ness is by usage known as aham-vritti, it is not really a vritti like the other vrittis of the mind. Because unlike the other vrittis which have no essential interrelation, the aham-vritti is equally and essentially related to each and every vritti of the mind. Without the aham-vritti there can be no other vritti, but the aham-vritti can subsist by itself without depending on any other vritti of the mind. The aham-vritti is therefore fundamentally different from other vrittis.

So then, the search for the source of the aham-vritti is not merely the search for the basis of one of the forms of the ego but for the very source itself from which arises the "I-am"-ness. In other words, the quest for and the realization of the source of the ego in the form of aham-vritti necessarily implies the transcendence of the ego in everyone of its possible forms.

Question: Conceding that the aham-vritti essentially comprises all the forms of the ego, why should that vritti alone be chosen as the means for self-inquiry?

Bhagavan: Because it is the one irreducible datum of your experience; because seeking its source is the only practicable course you can adopt to realize the Self. The ego is said to have a causal body [the state of the individual "I" in deep sleep], but how can you make it the subject of your investigation? When the ego adopts that form, you are immersed in the darkness of sleep.

Question: But is not the ego in its subtle [dream state] and causal [sleep state] forms too intangible to be tackled through the inquiry into the source of aham-vritti conducted while the mind is awake?

Bhagavan: No. The inquiry into the source of aham-vritti touches the very existence of the ego. Therefore the subtlety of the ego's form is not a material consideration.

Question: While the one aim is to realize the unconditioned, pure Being of the Self, which is in no way dependent on the ego, how can inquiry pertaining to the ego in the form of aham-vritti be of any use?

Bhagavan: From the functional point of view the form of … the ego has one and only one characteristic. The ego functions as the knot between the Self which is pure consciousness and the physical body which is inert and insentient. The ego is therefore called the chit-jada granthi [the knot between consciousness and the inert body]. In your investigation into the source of aham-vritti, you take the essential chit [consciousness] aspect of the ego: and for this reason the inquiry must lead to the realization of the pure consciousness of the Self.

Question: In the jnani [the enlightened being] the ego subsists in the sattvic [pure] form and therefore it appears as something real. Am I right?

Bhagavan: No. The existence of the ego in any form, either in the jnani or ajnani [unenlightened person], is itself an appearance. But to the ajnani who is deluded into thinking that the waking state and the world are real, the ego also appears to be real. Since he sees the jnani act like other individuals, he feels constrained to posit some notion of individuality with reference to the jnani also.

Question: How then does the aham-vritti function in the jnani?

Bhagavan: It does not function in him at all. The jnani's lakshya [target or spiritual focus] is the Heart itself, because he is one and identical with that undifferentiated, pure consciousness referred to by the Upanishads as the prajnana [complete consciousness]. Prajnana is verily Brahman [the impersonal absolute reality of Hinduism], the Absolute, and there is no Brahman other than prajnana.

Question: How then does ignorance of this one and only reality unhappily arise in the case of the ajnani [the unenlightened person]?

Bhagavan: The ajnani sees only the mind which is a mere reflection of the light of pure consciousness arising from the Heart. Of the Heart itself he is ignorant. Why? Because his mind is extroverted and has never sought its source.

Question: What prevents the infinite, undifferentiated light of consciousness arising from the Heart from revealing itself to the ajnani?

Bhagavan: Just as water in the pot reflects the enormous sun within the narrow limits of the pot, even so the vasanas or latent tendencies of the mind of the individual, acting as the reflecting medium, catch the all-pervading, infinite light of consciousness arising from the Heart and present, in the form of a reflection, the phenomenon called the mind. Seeing only this reflection, the ajnani is deluded into the belief that he is a finite being, the jiva.

If the mind becomes introverted through inquiry into the source of aham-vritti, the vasanas [mental tendencies and habits] become extinct, and in the absence of the reflecting medium, … the mind disappears, being absorbed into the light of the one reality, the Heart.

This is the sum and substance of all that an aspirant needs know. What is imperatively required of him is an earnest and one-pointed inquiry into the source of aham-vritti.

Self-inquiry is really possible only through intense introversion of the mind. What is finally realized as a result of such inquiry into the source of aham-vritti is verily the Heart as the undifferentiated light of pure Consciousness, into which the reflected light of the mind is completely absorbed.[14]

It is that reality that you should seek during your so-called waking state by tracing the aham-vritti to its source. Intense practice in this inquiry will reveal that the mind and its three states are unreal and that you are the eternal, infinite consciousness of pure Being, the Self or the Heart.[15]

Question: You say one can realize the Self by a search for it. What is the character of this search?

Bhagavan: You are the mind or think that you are the mind. The mind is nothing but thoughts. Now behind every particular thought there is a general thought which is the "I," that is yourself. Let us call this "I" the first thought. Stick to this "I"-thought and question it to find out what it is. When this question takes strong hold on you, you cannot think of other thoughts.

Question: When I do like this and cling to my self, i.e., the "I"-thought, other thoughts do come and go, but I say to myself "Who am I?" and there is no answer forthcoming. To be in this condition is the sadhana [spiritual practice]. Is it so?

Bhagavan: This is a mistake that people often make. What happens when you make a serious quest for the Self is that the "I"-thought as a thought disappears, and something else from the depths takes hold of you that is not the "I" which commenced the quest.

Question: What is this something else?

Bhagavan: That is the real Self, the import of "I." It is not the ego. It is the Supreme Being itself.

Question: But you have often said that one must reject other thoughts when one begins the quest, but the thoughts are endless; if one thought is rejected, another comes and there seems to be no end at all.

Bhagavan: I do not say that you must go on rejecting thoughts. If you cling to yourself, the "I"-thought, when your interest keeps you to that single idea, other thoughts get rejected, and automatically they vanish.

Question: And so rejection of thoughts is not necessary?

Bhagavan: No. It may be necessary for a time or for some. You fancy that there is no end if one goes on rejecting every thought when it rises. No. There is an end. If you are vigilant, and make a stern effort to reject every thought when it rises, you will soon find that you are going deeper and deeper into your own inner self, where there is no need for your effort to reject the thoughts.

Question: Then it is possible to be without effort, without strain!

Bhagavan: Not only that, it is impossible for you to make an effort beyond a certain extent.

Question: I want to be further enlightened. Should I try to make no effort at all?

Bhagavan: Here it is impossible for you to be without effort. When you go deeper, it is impossible for you to make any effort.

Question: Then I can dispense with outside help and by mine own effort get into the deeper truth by myself.

Bhagavan: True. But the very fact that you are possessed of the quest of the Self is a manifestation of the divine grace. It is effulgent in the Heart, the inner being, the real Self. It draws you from within. You have to attempt to get in from without. Your attempt is vichara [inquiry], the deep inner movement is grace. That is why I say there is no real vichara without grace, nor is there grace active for him who is without vichara. Both are necessary.[16]

Question: If I go on rejecting thoughts can I call it vichara?

Bhagavan: It may be a stepping stone. But really vichara begins when you cling to your Self and are already off the mental movement, the thought-waves.

Question: Then vichara is not intellectual?

Bhagavan: No, it is anthara vichara, inner quest.[17]

Question: What is dhyana [meditation]?

Bhagavan: It is abiding as the Self without swerving even slightly from the state of the Self in any of the avasthas [the three states of waking, dreaming and sleeping], and without giving room for even the thought "I am meditating."...

Question: What is the difference between dhyana and samadhi [a trance-like absorption in the Self]?

Bhagavan: Dhyana is imagination of the mind, made through one's own effort; in samadhi there is no such effort.

Question: What are the factors to be kept in view in dhyana?

Bhagavan: It is important for one who is established in his Self to see that he does not swerve in the least from this one-pointed absorption. While swerving from his true nature he may see before him bright effulgences, etc., or hear unusual sounds or regard as real the visions of gods appearing within or outside himself. He should not be deceived by these and forget himself.[18]

Question: What are the rules of conduct which an aspirant should follow?

Bhagavan: Moderation in food, moderation in sleep and moderation in speech.

Question: How long should one practice?

Bhagavan: Until the mind attains effortlessly its natural state of freedom from concepts, that is, till the sense of "I" and "mine" are totally destroyed.

Question: If everything happens according to prarabdha karma [the predestined script of one's life], how is one to overcome the obstacles to meditation?

Bhagavan: Prarabdha concerns only the out-turned, not the inturned mind. One who seeks his real Self will not be afraid of any obstacle. The thought of an obstacle is itself the greatest obstacle.[19]

Question: How can I get peace? I do not seem to obtain it through vichara [inquiry].

Bhagavan: Peace is your natural state. It is the mind that obstructs the natural state. Your vichara has been made only in the mind. Investigate what the mind is, and it will disappear. There is no such thing as mind apart from thought. Nevertheless, because of the emergence of thought, you surmise something from which it starts and term that the mind. When you probe to see what it is, you find there is really no such thing as mind. When the mind has thus vanished, you realize eternal peace.[20]

If you strengthen the mind, that peace will continue for all time. Its duration is proportional to the strength of mind acquired by repeated practice. And such a mind is able to hold on to the current. In that case, engagement or no engagement in work, the current remains unaffected and uninterrupted. It is not the work that hinders but the idea that it is you who are doing it.

Question: Is a set meditation necessary for strengthening the mind?

Bhagavan: Not if you keep the idea always before you that it is not your work. At first, effort is needed to remind yourself of it, but later on it becomes natural and continuous. The work will go on of its own accord, and your peace will remain undisturbed.

Meditation is your true nature. You call it meditation now, because there are other thoughts distracting you. When these thoughts are dispelled, you remain alone—that is, in the state of meditation free from thoughts. That is your real nature, which you are now trying to gain by keeping away other thoughts. Such keeping away of other thoughts is now called meditation. But when the practice becomes firm, the real nature shows itself as true meditation.[21]

Some of the passages used in this chapter have been translated directly from the original Tamil work, *Upadesa Manjari*, by T. V. Venkatasubramanian and David Godman.

On Practice

Bhagavan Sri Ramana Maharshi

We have mentioned the two ways to turn our attention. Bhagavan considers them more fully in this chapter. He says, "There are two ways; one is looking into the source of 'I' and merging into that source. The other is feeling 'I am helpless by myself, God alone is all-powerful and except throwing myself completely on him, there is no other means of safety for me,' thus gradually developing the conviction that God alone exists and the ego does not count. Both methods lead to the same goal."

By the end of this chapter we will have further deepened our understanding of nonduality and how to realize the Self or nondual nature. Then we will be able to further appreciate and understand confessions, writings, teachings, scriptures from major world religions, which is what the next part of this book is about.

Bhagavan: That from which the "I"-thought, the first thought, rises is the Heart, the Self, consciousness of being. Pursue in the Heart the inquiry "Who is this 'I' that is the source for the manifestation of the ego and all the rest?"[1]

That which arises in the physical body as "I" is the mind. If one enquires, "In what place in the body does this 'I' first arise?" it will be known to be in the Heart. That is the birthplace of the mind. Even if one incessantly thinks "I, I," it will lead to that place. Of all thoughts that arise in the mind, the thought "I" is the first one. It is only after the rise of this [thought] that other thoughts arise. It is only after the first personal pronoun arises that the second and third personal pronouns appear. Without the first person, the second and third persons cannot exist.[2]

The Heart is used in the Vedas and the scriptures to denote the place whence the notion "I" springs. Does it spring only from the fleshy ball? It springs within us somewhere right in the middle of our being. The "I" has no location. Everything is the Self. There is nothing but that. So, the Heart must be said to be the entire body of ourselves and of the entire universe, conceived as "I." But to help the practiser [abhyasi] we have to indicate a definite part of the universe, or of the body. So this Heart is pointed out as the seat of the Self. But in truth we are everywhere, we are all that is, and there is nothing else.[3]

Until one enquires into and knows one's own real nature, the agitation experienced by the mind will not cease. For your true state to merge in your Heart as your own nature, you must enquire and know that true state. This is the only way.

Those who leave the path of self-inquiry, the way of liberation, and wander off along the myriad forest tracks, will encounter only confusion. The state of the Self is reached by going back the way one came. Whatever other paths one travels on, it has to take you here and take refuge here.[4]

This path is the direct path; all others are indirect ways. The first leads to the Self, the others elsewhere. And even if the latter do arrive at the Self it is only because they lead at the end to the first path which ultimately carries them to the goal. So, in the end, the aspirants must adopt the first path. Why not do so now? Why waste time?[5]

Do not ruin yourself by repeatedly rising and subsiding as the thinking "I." Attain true life by abiding as the being "I."[6]

Question: This "I"-thought rises from me. But I do not know the Self.

Bhagavan: All these are only mental concepts. You are now identifying yourself with a wrong "I," which is the "I"-thought. This "I"-thought rises and sinks, whereas the true significance of "I" is beyond both. There cannot be a break in your being. You who slept are also now awake. There was not unhappiness in your deep sleep. Whereas it exists now. What is it that has happened now so that this difference is experienced? There was no "I"-thought in your sleep, whereas it is present now. The true "I" is not apparent and the false "I" is parading itself. This false "I" is the obstacle to your right knowledge. Find out wherefrom this false "I" arises. Then it will disappear. You will be only what you are—i.e. absolute being.

Question: How to do it? I have not succeeded so far.

Bhagavan: Search for the source of the "I"-thought. That is all that one has to do. The universe exists on account of the

"I"-thought. If that ends there is an end of misery also. The false "I" will end only when its source is sought.[7]

Prevent and stop the "I"-thought from arising and attaching itself to any *upadhi* [false identification]. To remain naturally merged in the Heart, without rising as "I," is the proper *dharma.*

To enquire and know oneself properly, nothing except the consciousness "I am" is necessary.[8]

Question: How is that to be done?

Bhagavan: The questioner must admit the existence of his self. "I am" is the realization. To pursue the clue till realization is vichara [inquiry]. Vichara and realization are the same.

Question: It is elusive. What shall I meditate upon?

Bhagavan: Meditation requires an object to meditate upon, whereas there is only the subject without the object in vichara. Meditation differs from vichara in this way…

Question: Will vichara alone do in the absence of meditation?

Bhagavan: Vichara is the process and the goal also. "I am" is the goal and the final reality. To hold to it with effort is vichara. When spontaneous and natural it is realization.[9]

To enable the sadhaka [seeker] to steer clear of possible doubt, I tell him to take up the "thread" or the clue of "I"-ness or "I-am"-ness and follow it up to its source. Because, firstly, it is impossible for anybody to entertain any doubt about his "I"-notion; secondly whatever be the sadhana [practice] adopted, the final goal is the realization of the source of "I-am"-ness which is the primary datum of your experience.

If you, therefore, practise atma-vichara [self-inquiry] you will reach the Heart, which is the Self.[10]

"I exist" is the only permanent, self-evident experience of everyone. Nothing else is so self-evident [pratyaksha] as "I am." What people call self-evident viz., the experience they get through the senses, is far from self-evident. The Self alone is that. Pratyaksha is another name for the Self. So, to do self-analysis and be "I am" is the only thing to do. "I am" is reality. I am this or that is unreal. "I am" is truth, another name for Self.[11]

Question: Please say how I shall realize the "I." Am I to make the japa [repetition of the phrase] "Who am I?"

Bhagavan: No japa of the kind is meant.

Question: Am I to think "Who am I?"

Bhagavan: You have known that the "I"-thought springs forth. Hold the "I"-thought and find its moola [source].

Question: May I know the way?

Bhagavan: Do as you have now been told and see.

Question: I do not understand what I should do.

Bhagavan: If it is anything objective the way can be shown objectively. This is subjective.

Question: But I do not understand.

Bhagavan: What! Do you not understand that you are?

Question: Please tell me the way.

Bhagavan: Is it necessary to show the way in the interior of your own home? This is within you.[12]

Stop thinking and know by careful investigation only the reality that is within your Heart as your own nature. Letting go of external objects, turn your back on them, and realize through keen inquiry the effulgent truth that shines in the Heart.

The answer to the question "Who am I?" is only the silent jnana that shines as "I-I" in the Heart.[13]

Questioning "Who am I?" within one's mind, when one reaches the Heart, the individual "I" sinks crestfallen, and at once reality manifests itself as "I-I." Though it reveals itself thus, it is not the ego "I" but the perfect being, the Self Absolute.[14]

That which shines as "I-I" in the Heart, mauna [silence], the real nature of true jnana, is itself liberation. Do not imagine that there are two "I"s and suffer and lament as a consequence. By consolidating yourself in the Self, know and enjoy the "I" as one. Do not perish amidst all your troubles but recognise your target to be the truth of the Self that dwells as "I" within your Heart; cling to it and attain the bliss of consciousness.[15]

Question: If "I" also be an illusion, who then casts off the illusion?

Bhagavan: The "I" casts off the illusion of "I" and yet remains as "I." Such is the paradox of Self-realization. The realized do not see any contradiction in it. Take the case of bhakti [devotion]. I approach Iswara [God] and pray to be absorbed in Him. I then surrender myself in faith and by concentration. What remains afterwards? In place of the original "I," perfect self-surrender leaves a residuum of God in which the "I" is lost. This is the highest form of devotion [parabhakti], prapatti, surrender, or the height of vairagya [detachment].

You give up this and that of "my" possessions. If you give up "I" and "mine" instead, all are given up at a stroke. The very seed of possession is lost. Thus the evil is nipped in the bud or crushed in the germ itself. Dispassion must be very strong to do this. Eagerness to do it must be equal to that of a man kept under water trying to rise up to the surface for his life.[16]

There are two ways; one is looking into the source of "I" and merging into that source. The other is feeling "I am helpless by myself, God alone is all-powerful and except throwing myself completely on him, there is no other means of safety for me," thus gradually developing the conviction that God alone exists and the ego does not count. Both methods lead to the same goal. Complete surrender is another name for jnana or liberation.[17]

Offer yourself up unconditionally to the power that is your own source.[18]

It is enough that one surrenders oneself. Surrender is to give oneself up to the original cause of one's being. Do not delude yourself by imagining such a source to be some God outside you. Your source is within yourself. Give yourself up to it. That means that you should seek the source and merge in it.[19]

Surrender can take effect only when it is done with full knowledge as to what real surrender means. Such knowledge comes after inquiry and reflection and ends invariably in self-surrender. There is no difference between jnana and absolute surrender to the Lord, that is, in thought, word and deed.[20]

Since to renounce the ego is to offer up one's self in surrender, cast out the debased ego-mind that proclaims itself to be "I." This destruction of the ego, this loss of individuality—a state in which attachment to the non-Self does not find a foothold—is self-surrender. To be absorbed, through surrender of the Self, in the non-dual state of mauna, [silence] is the supreme truth. That which constitutes offering [oneself] up to the Self is living the life that shines, free of the false delusive mind, known as "I."[21]

Question: Surrender is impossible.

Bhagavan: Yes. Complete surrender is impossible in the beginning. Partial surrender is certainly possible for all. In course of time that will lead to complete surrender. Well, if surrender is impossible, what can be done? There is no peace of mind. You are helpless to bring it about. It can be done only by surrender.[22]

Question: Does not total or complete surrender require that one should not have left in him the desire even for liberation or God?

Bhagavan: Complete surrender does require that you have no desire of your own, that God's desire alone is your desire and that you have no desire of your own.[23]

Banish even the thought "I am a fit instrument for Him" and remain still [summa iru].[24]

Abidance in one's real state is ceasing to exist as a slave [of God]; it is remaining without even the thought "I am a slave" rising; it is egoless mauna [silence], utterly still, having no mental movements. The unlimited consciousness that shines in this state is the [true] consciousness.[25]

Surrender to Him and abide by His will whether he appears or vanishes; await His pleasure. If you ask Him to do as *you* please, it is not surrender but command to Him. You cannot have Him obey you and yet think that you have surrendered. He knows what is best and when and how to do it. Leave everything to Him. His is the burden; you have no longer any cares. All your cares are His. Such is surrender. This is bhakti.

Or, enquire to whom these questions arise. Dive deep in the Heart and remain as the Self. One of these two ways is open to the aspirant.[26]

Part Three

Nondual Confessions

Now we'll look at scriptural and confessional texts that are nondual in their sensibility. The hunger for nonduality has turned to self-realization and now to confession of what nondual recognition is about. These writings can be viewed as songs to Self or God.

These confessions are not grounded in mystical experiences that came and went, leaving a strong memory of a momentary recognition of nondual reality. Rather, they arise out of the ground of permanent and continuous realization of the Self.

Glimpses of the Self, the Absolute, or whatever one wishes to call it, are not uncommon. Certainly such glimpses can be beneficial in life. They give us a bigger perspective on day-to-day living and therefore ease our suffering. Memory of mystical experience can bring a measure of peace. What may arise is an awareness of and detachment from what John Wren-Lewis called "a collective nightmare of separate individuals struggling in an alien universe for survival, satisfaction and significance."[1]

Like the desire for nonduality, transient experiences of the Self arrive "through the grace of God alone."[2]

These confessors, with their madness about nonduality, Self, or God, come from a variety of traditions, briefly described here.

ADVAITA VEDANTA

From Advaita Vedanta comes Dattatreya, supposedly the author of the *Avadhuta Gita*. "*The Avadhuta Gita* is … written in spirited Sanskrit verse, which breathes the atmosphere of the highest experience of Brahman [Hindu name for God or Self]. It goes into no philosophical argument to prove oneness of reality, but is content to make the most startling statements, leaving the seeker of truth to imbibe them and be lifted from illusion into the blazing light of Knowledge (jnana)."[3]

In the *Avadhuta Gita* we see Dattatreya blaze: "I, the One only, am all this, beyond space and continuous. How can I see the Self as visible or hidden? … Thus you are One. Why then do you not understand that you are the unchangeable One, equally perceived in all? O mighty One, how can you, who are ever-shining, unrestricted, think of day and night?"[4]

SUFISM

About the Sufi Ibn 'Arabi it is said, "All his life [he] felt the pain of not being understood. Yet the breadth and depth of his wisdom, insight, vision, and knowledge was and is awesome to whomever catches a glimpse of it. Many of his expressions of divine mysteries have never been improved upon."[5]

Listen to a few lines of Ibn 'Arabi's confession in which Allah is called "He," and which could be called Self or God for purposes of this book:

> He is the First without anything before Him. He is the Last without anything after Him. He is Visible in all that is seen. He is Known, clearly, in all that is hidden. He is in all forms and images without any relation to any appearance. He is the secret and the appearance of the first letter announcing the beginning of existence. He is the presence of all the letters that belong to the First and all the letters that belong

to the Last and is the presence in all the letters that are visible and all the letters that are hidden.

May Allah have mercy on the soul of Muhyiddin Ibn 'Arabi, and may He be pleased with him and bestow peace upon his soul.

Such confessions come forth when the desire for nonduality is turned toward inquiry or surrender. With such intensity, existence as the Self is known, perceived, and experienced, whether or not passionate written description emerges.

JUDAISM

Though the authors of the Kabbalah of Judaism are not known, we hear the spirit of the song of the free: "The depth of primordial being is called Boundless. Because of its concealment from all creatures above and below, it is also called Nothingness. If one asks, 'What is it?' the answer is, 'Nothing.'"[6] This is a bold statement characteristic of the self-realized one.

TAOISM

The Tao Te Ching is widely known as the classic philosophical and scriptural text of Taoism. Though Lao Tzu is the named author, Victor H. Mair, editor of the version excerpted here, states that this Taoist text "represents the accumulated wisdom of centuries, not the enterprise of one author."[7]

To realize that you do not understand is a virtue;
Not to realize that you do not understand is a defect.

The reason why
The sage has no defects,
Is because he treats defects as defects.

Thus,
He has no defects.[8]

NATIVE AMERICAN TRADITION

Kent Nerburn tells us about the Native American writer Ohiyesa, "He was ever the observer, journeying ever deeper into the ways of white culture, trying, as his grandmother had always instructed him, 'to follow a new trail to the point of knowing.' The writings he has left are the documents of that journey, crafted by a man with a warrior's heart, an orator's tongue, and human spirit of such dignity that it transcends boundaries of race and belief."[9] Ohiyesa wrote:

> We believe profoundly in silence—the sign of a perfect equilibrium. Silence is the absolute poise or balance of body, mind, and spirit. Those who can preserve their selfhood ever calm and unshaken by the storms of existence—not a leaf, as it were, astir on the tree; not a ripple upon the shining pool—those, in the mind of the person of nature, possess the ideal attitude and conduct of life.
>
> If you ask us, "What is silence?" we will answer, "It is the Great Mystery. The holy silence is God's voice."
>
> If you ask, "What are the fruits of silence?" we will answer, "They are self-control, true courage or endurance, patience, dignity, and reverence. Silence is the cornerstone of character."[10]

CHRISTIANITY

The chapter on nondual Christianity is challenging and extreme. In the life and teaching of Bernadette Roberts we meet a Christian apophatic contemplative. "Bernadette Roberts is the first advanced contemplative to psychologically describe complete human transformation in the Divine: first as the ego falls away, then followed by the self's unconscious dissolution, and finally self's ultimate end."[11]

Roberts confesses, "In order to come upon Eternal Form, all form must first be an absolute void where nothing can possibly be relative to it; it is only from this position that Eternal Form can be revealed. By definition the divine or Absolute is 'that' which is nonrelative, and the only thing that can be nonrelative is a void of voids.

This void of voids or absolute nothing IS Christ."[12]

BUDDHISM

"If you meet the Buddha, kill the Buddha!" is a Zen teaching emphasizing focus upon the Self and nothing outward: not authorities, teachers, visions, hopes and dreams, ideas, experiences, or the works of self-realized people. The Buddhist scripture the Diamond Sutra is, like the confession of Bernadette Roberts, difficult to grasp:

> The essential doctrine of the Diamond Sutra is that no sort or kind of self is to be considered as existing. Having disposed of the I-concept, the Buddha proceeds to dispose of the elements that serve as the basis for it. . . .
>
> In short, as Hui Neng realized so early in life, nothing at all exists, which is the Void. But the Buddha always adds that therefore everything exists in some manner.[13]

We may wish to explore the confession that nothing at all exists and therefore everything exists. To have one without the other means that life is not going to be lived effectively. In one scenario we'll be sitting in an alley with everything imaginable crawling over us while we exist as the Absolute. In another, we'll be running frantically to and away from this and that in order to accomplish something that we think is important. The topic of nothing and everything existing at the same time will be addressed at the end of this book. However, hints and instruction on the topic will be found at places throughout the chapters in this part.

RELATING TO THESE WRITINGS AND TO SELF-REALIZED PEOPLE

It is not necessary to fully understand what Roberts or any of these people—is saying. It is important to grasp that self-realized people are speaking from an understanding about reality very different from the understanding of most others. Also, this quality of understanding has roots in the desire for nonduality and the attentional acts of inquiry and surrender.

Not only are these authors self-realized, but they are also extraordinary communicators. Not every self-realized person is writing scriptural quality texts or great poetry. We might respect and be in awe of these authors because they are gifted humans. However, the talents, gifts, works, and experiences belonging to another, or belonging to ourselves for that matter, have nothing to do with following our desire for nonduality.

Our desire is for nonduality, not to be recognized as a poet, writer, teacher, speaker, guru. We may become one of those people, but our objective is otherwise. We could just as well be living out of our car and doing odd jobs.

Recall Sri Ramana Maharshi's words: "It is important for one who is established in his Self to see that he does not swerve in the least from this one-pointed absorption. While swerving from his true nature he may see before him bright effulgences, etc., or hear unusual sounds or regard as real the visions of gods appearing within or outside himself. He should not be deceived by these and forget himself."[14]

OUR REAL JOB

We have heard samplings of a few very diverse "songs" about to be played. Some will be familiar, some will be agreeably challenging, others will be strange and possibly disturbing. What seems difficult to understand today may suddenly become clear another day.

While reading, periodically we return to what we understand: the desire for nonduality, the nature of Self, truth, or nondual reality; the practice of inquiry, the act of surrender. Attending to what we know as our deepest, most fundamental self, or allowing our understanding of Self to unfold, could be considered our purpose in this life. We could say that our purpose is the fulfillment of our desire for nonduality, or recognition that there is no separation from Self.

The readings in this section arise out of accomplishment of this single purpose, but we shall see that it is not completely accurate to say that one accomplishes the purpose. We come to understand that there is no separation between us and purpose, between us and Self.

ADVAITA VEDANTA
The Avadhuta Gita

Dattatreya

INTRODUCTION BY SWAMI ASHOKANANDA

The *Avadhuta Gita* is a text of Vedanta representing extreme Advaita or Nondualism. It is ascribed to Dattatreya (Datta, son of Atri), who is looked upon as an Incarnation of God. Unfortunately, we possess no historical data concerning when or where he was born, how long he lived, or how he arrived at the knowledge disclosed in the text. Some of the Puranas [ancient Hindu narratives] mention him, and of these, the *Markandeya* contains the longest reference; but even this is legendary and by no means very informative.

The account in the *Markandeya Purana* suggests the following facts of Dattatreya's life: He was born of highly spiritual parents, Atri and Anasuya; very early in life he became renowned as a great warrior, and soon, renouncing the world and devoting himself to the practice of yoga, he attained to the highest state of liberation, thus becoming an *avadhuta*.

Avadhuta means a liberated soul, one who has "passed away from" or "shaken off" all worldly attachments and cares and has attained a spiritual state equivalent to the existence of God. Though avadhuta naturally implies renunciation, it includes an additional and yet higher state which is neither attachment nor detachment but beyond both. An avadhuta feels no need of observing any rules, either secular or religious. He seeks nothing, avoids nothing. He has neither knowledge nor ignorance. Having realized that he is the infinite Self, he lives in that vivid realization. To the Hindu mind, Dattatreya is a symbol of this realization. …

The *Avadhuta Gita* is a small book of only eight chapters and is written in spirited Sanskrit verse, which breathes the atmosphere of the highest experience of Brahman. It goes into no philosophical argument to prove oneness of reality, but is content to make the most startling statements, leaving the seeker of truth to imbibe them and be lifted from illusion into the blazing light of Knowledge (jnana).

Advaita Vedantins have prized this *Gita* highly. Swami Vivekananda, one of the greatest Advaitans of all time, often quoted from this *Gita*. He once said, "Men like the one who wrote this Song keep religion alive. They have actually realized; they care for nothing, feel nothing done to the body, care not for heat, cold, danger, or anything. They sit still, enjoying the bliss of Atman, and though red-hot coals burn the body, they feel them not."

THE AVADHUTA GITA (VERSES 1 – 41)

1. Through the grace of God alone, the desire for nonduality arises in wise men to save them from great fear.

2. How shall I salute the formless Being, indivisible, auspicious, and immutable, who fills all this with His Self and also fills the self with His Self?

3. The universe composed of the five elements is like water in a mirage. Oh, to whom shall I make obeisance—I who am one and taintless?

4. All is verily the absolute Self. Distinction and nondistinction do not exist. How can I say, "It exists; it does not exist?" I am filled with wonder!

5. The essence and the whole of Vedanta is this Knowledge, this supreme Knowledge: that I am by nature the formless, all-pervasive Self.

6. There is no doubt that I am that God who is the Self of all, pure, indivisible, like the sky, naturally stainless.

7. I indeed am immutable and infinite and of the form of pure Intelligence. I do not know how or in relation to whom Joy and sorrow exist.

8. I have no mental activity, good or bad; I have no bodily function, good or bad; I have no verbal action, good or bad. I am the nectar of Knowledge, beyond the senses, pure.

9. The mind indeed is of the form of space. The mind indeed is omnifaced. The mind is the past. The mind is all. But in reality there is no mind.

10. I, the One only, am all this, beyond space and continuous. How can I see the Self as visible or hidden?

11. Thus you are One. Why then do you not understand that you are the unchangeable One, equally perceived in all? O mighty One, how can you, who are ever-shining, unrestricted, think of day and night?

12. Know the Self always to be everywhere, one and unintercepted. I am the meditator and the highest object of meditation. Why do you divide the indivisible?

13. You are not born nor do you die. At no time do you have a body. The scripture declares in many different ways the well-known dictum: "All is Brahman."

14. You are He who is exterior and interior. You are the auspicious One existing everywhere at all times. Why are you running hither and thither deluded, like an unclean spirit?

15. Union and separation exist in regard neither to you nor to me. There is no you, no me, nor is there this universe. All is verily the Self alone.

16. You do not belong to that which is composed of the five objects of sense, such as sound; nor does that belong to you. You indeed are the supreme Reality. Why then do you suffer?

17. For you there is no birth or death, for you there is mind, for you there is no bondage or liberation, no good or evil. Why do you shed tears, my child? Neither you nor I have name and form.

18. O mind, why do you wander about deluded, like an unclean spirit? Behold the Self indivisible. Be happy through renunciation of attachment.

19. You verily are Truth, devoid of change, motionless, one, of the nature of freedom. You have neither attachment nor aversion. Why do you suffer, seeking the objects of desires?

20. All the scriptures say that the Truth is without attributes, pure, immutable, bodiless, and existing equally everywhere. Know me to be That. There is not the least doubt about it.

21. Know that which has form to be false, that which is formless to be eternal. Through the instruction of this truth there is no longer rebirth into this world.

22. Sages say that Reality is one only and the same. And through renunciation of attachment, the mind, which is one and many, ceases to exist.

23. If it is of the nature of the not-Self, how can there be samadhi (superconscious realization)? If it is of the nature of the Self, how can there be samadhi? If it is both "is" and "is not," how can there be samadhi? If all is one and of the nature of freedom, how can there be samadhi?

24. You are pure homogeneous Reality, disembodied, unborn, and immutable. Why do you think of yourself as "I know it here" or as "I do not know"?

25. By such sentences as "That thou art," your own Self is affirmed. Of that which is untrue and composed of the five elements the Sruti says, "Not this, not this."

26. As the self is filled by the Self, so is all filled continuously by you. There is no meditator or meditation. Why does your mind meditate shamelessly?

27. I do not know the Supreme; how shall I speak of Him? I do not know the Supreme; how shall I worship Him? If I am the supreme One, who is the highest Truth, who is homogeneous Being and like unto space, how then shall I speak of Him and worship Him?

28. The principle of ego is not the Truth, which is homogeneous, which is free from the cause of superimposition and distinctions of perceived and perceiver. How can the ego be That which is aware of Itself?

29. There is no substance whatever which is by nature unlimited. There is no substance whatever which is of the nature of Reality. The very Self is the supreme Truth. There is neither injury nor noninjury of It.

30. You are the homogeneous Reality; you are pure, bodiless, birthless, and imperishable. Why then do you have any delusion about the Self? Again, why am I myself deluded?

31. When the pot is broken, the space within it is absorbed in the infinite space and becomes undifferentiated. When the mind

becomes pure, I do not perceive any difference between the mind and the supreme Being.

32. There is no pot; there is no pot's interior space. Neither is there an individual soul nor the form of an individual soul. Know the absolute Brahman, devoid of knowable and knower.

33. Know me to be that Self who is everything and everywhere at all times, who is eternal, steady, the All, the nonexistent, and the Existent. Have no doubt.

34. There are no Vedas, no worlds, no gods, no sacrifices. There is certainly no caste, no stage in life, no family, no birth. There is neither the path of smoke nor the path of light. There is only the highest Truth, the homogeneous Brahman.

35. If you are free of the pervaded and the pervader, if you are one and fulfilled, how can you think of yourself as directly perceptible by the senses or beyond the range of the senses?

36. Some seek nonduality, others duality. They do not know the Truth, which is the same at all times and everywhere, which is devoid of both duality and nonduality.

37. How can they describe the Truth, which is beyond the mind and words, which is devoid of white and other colours, of sound and other qualities?

38. When all these appear to you as false, when the body and so on appear to you like space, then you know Brahman truly, then for you there is no dual series.

39. Even my natural self appears to me as non-distinct from the Supreme Self; it appears to be one and like space. How can there be meditator and meditation?

40. What I do, what I eat, what I sacrifice, what I give—all this is not mine in the least. I am pure, unborn, undecaying.

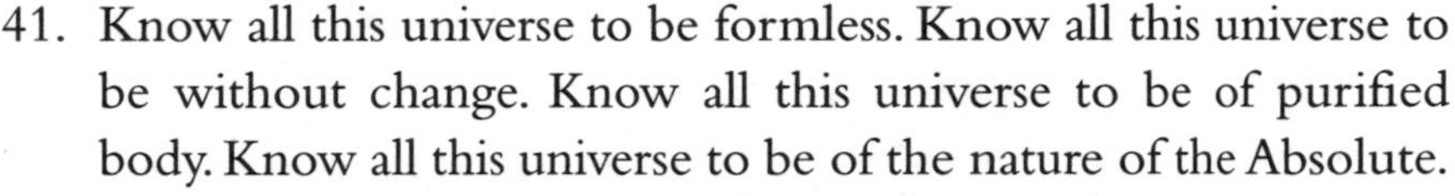

41. Know all this universe to be formless. Know all this universe to be without change. Know all this universe to be of purified body. Know all this universe to be of the nature of the Absolute.

SUFISM
The One Alone

Ibn 'Arabi

INTRODUCTION BY SHAYKH TOSUN BAYRAK AL-JERRAHI AL-HALVETI

Ibn 'Arabi all his life felt the pain of not being understood. Yet the breadth and depth of his wisdom, insight, vision, and knowledge was and is awesome to whomever catches a glimpse of it. Many of his expressions of divine mysteries have never been improved upon. Many important affairs, which he foretold centuries ago, have taken place and continue to take place.

Despite—or because of—the controversy surrounding him, Ibn 'Arabi has become one of the most important expounders of Sufi wisdom. His influences quickly spread even beyond the Islamic world, entering medieval Europe. In their famous studies, Asin Palacios and Salverda di Grave have pointed out that Dante, in the *Divina Comedia* was often inspired by Ibn 'Arabi's works, deriving from them both the grand design of Hell and Paradise and the image of the beautiful young woman as guide to the divine. Through Dante's prestige, these themes permeated old Europe. Today, the Shaikh's influence on the spiritual growth of humanity continues to grow as his words become more and more available in the West.

In his prime, Ibn 'Arabi was a thin, middle-sized man—well proportioned, with small, delicate hands and feet. His skin was white. His head was small, with a round face, a high forehead and a fine slightly curved nose of medium size. He had eyebrows curved like the crescent moon; he wore a thick white beard.

He was courageous and tenacious, extremely patient, and very generous with both the material things he owned and the deep wisdom he possessed.

Although not everyone understood him, all were in awe of his spiritual presence. Always gentle, compassionate, and merciful, he viewed everything with love, including his enemies and dangerous animals. He detested violence, even in the punishment of murderers. He wrote, "Although according to religious law the punishment for murder is death, it is better to forgive." He also wrote, "On the Day of Judgment, I will intercede for those who deny me."

Muhyiddin Abu Bakr Muhammad ibn 'al-'Arabi was born on August 7, 1165 (560H), on the twenty-seventh day of Ramadan, in the city of Murcia in Andalusia. He was a descendant of Hatim at-Ta'i, the legendary model of Arab generosity.

He left this world on the night of Friday, November 16, 1240 (638H), the twenty-eighth day of the Arabic month of Rabi' ath Thani. He was seventy-six years old.

May Allah have mercy on the soul of Muhyiddin Ibn 'Arabi, and may He be pleased with him and bestow peace upon his soul.

THE ONE ALONE

In the Name of Allah the Merciful,
the One Who is visible
with all His beautiful names and attributes
in the realm of images.

"He who knows himself, knows his Lord."

All praise and thanks to Allah, Almighty, the first with no other before Him. He is the only First, and there is no last but His oneness. The end is with Him alone, and He is the end. He is All-Existing: with Him there is no end. Neither is there nearness or farness; nor is there a will or wish, or time, or above, or below, or place; neither is there a universe. Allah is now as He was before. He is eternal. He is One without oneness and Alone without loneliness. He is not named with a name, for it is He whose name is "He," the self-named one. There is no name other than "He," and none other than He is named.

He is the First without anything before Him. He is the Last without anything after Him. He is Visible in all that is seen. He is Known, clearly, in all that is hidden. He is in all forms and images without any relation to any appearance. He is the secret and the appearance of the first letter announcing the beginning of existence. He is the presence of all the letters that belong to the First and all the letters that belong to the Last and is the presence in all the letters that are visible and all the letters that are hidden. Therefore He is "the First" and "the Last" and "the Visible" and "the Hidden." He is the First and the Last and the Visible and the Hidden. All the letters that form the words, from the first to the last of realms seen or unseen, are without any relation to His Being and are without any effect on His Being.

Do not fall into the blasphemous error of the sect called Huluiyyah, who believe that another soul, even another being, can be infused into them and that they may have God materially existing in them. Know that He is never in anything, nor is anything in Him. He is neither inside nor outside of anything. None can see Him, whether with the eyes of the head or with an inner eye; nor can any conceive Him through the senses, the mind, intelligence, knowledge, or imagination. Only He can see Himself; only He can conceive Himself. None can know Him; only He can know Himself. He sees Himself by Himself; He conceives Himself by Himself; He knows Himself by Himself. None other than He can see Him. None other than He can know Him. That which hides Him is His oneness. None but himself can hide Him. The veil that hides Him is His own being. He hides His being with nothing other than His being the Only One; therefore, none other than He can see Him.

Neither a prophet whom He has sent to humanity, nor a saint, a perfect man, nor an angel close to Him can see Him, for they are not apart from Him. His prophets, His messengers, His perfect men, are none other than He, for He has sent Himself, from Himself, for Himself, without any other cause or means besides Himself. He sent His essence, from His essence, by His essence, to His essence. There is no difference between the One who sent and His messengers who were sent. The letters of His being are the being of His messengers. There is no other being than He. Neither does He become another; nor does His name become another's name; nor is there any other named by His name.

That is why our Master, the Light of the Universe, the Prophet Muhammad (may Allah's peace and blessing be upon him), said:

> I know my Lord by my Lord.

He also said:

> He who knows himself knows his Lord.

By this it is meant that surely you are not you, and you—without being you—are He. He is not within you; nor are you in Him. He does not exclude you; nor are you excluded from Him. When you are addressed as you, do not think that you exist, with an essence and qualities and attributes—for you never existed, nor do exist, nor will ever exist. You have not entered into Him, nor He into you. Without being, your essence is with Him and in Him. You were not; nor are you temporal. Without having any identity, you are Him and He is you. If you know yourself as nothing, then you truly know your Lord. Otherwise, you know Him not.

You cannot know your Lord by making yourself nothing. Many a wise man claims that in order to know one's Lord one must denude oneself of the signs of one's existence, efface one's identity, finally rid oneself of one's self. This is a mistake. How could a thing that does not exist try to get rid of its existence? For none of matter exists. How could a thing that is not, become nothing? A thing can only become nothing after it has been something. Therefore, if you know yourself without being, not trying to become nothing, you will know your Lord. If you think that to know Allah depends on your ridding yourself of yourself, then you are guilty of attributing partners to Him—the only unforgivable sin—because you are claiming that there is another existence besides Him, the All-Existent: that there is a you and a He.

Our Master, the Prophet (peace and blessings be upon him), said:

> He who knows himself knows His Lord.

He did not say:

> He who eliminates himself knows his Lord!

The proof of the existence of something is that when it is presumed nonexistent, its opposite appears. As there is none other than Allah, proving His existence does not depend on the disappearance of some existence other than His. And as you do not exist, you cannot cease to exist, nor be transformed into anything else. Your being is neither temporal nor eternal, for you have no being.

Our Master, the Messenger of Allah, said, "Actually you do not exist, as you did not exist before you were created."

Allah has no partners and there is none like unto Him.

Allah Most High is the meaning of before the before and after the after; without Him, before and after have no meaning. Were this not so,

He is alone. He has no partners.

would have no meaning. It must be so; otherwise something other than He would have to exist on its own and not depend on Him for its existence. Such a partner would not need Allah for its existence and so would be a second god—and that is an impossibility. Allah Most High cannot have partners, and there cannot be any like unto Him.

If one believes that things exist in Allah—from Him or with Him—and that these things depend upon Allah for their existence, even so, such things are appearing to one as lords. Though their lordship may depend on Allah, still one who believes in them is guilty of recognizing some other lord as a partner of our Lord. It would be a grave error to consider any other existence as valid alongside of Allah the Self-Existent, even if the thing is seen as dependent on Allah for its existence. A being that has given up its existence and has become naught after having given up its existence, is still far from a breath of knowledge.

If one contemplates oneself as such a being, one is far from knowing oneself. If someone thinks of himself as existing among other beings and things that disappear as he does, whose nothingness becomes naught in nothing—if such a person believes that there are others who exist beside Allah, he is nothing indeed, and his nothingness will go on as long as he thinks he exists. He will be guilty of the unforgivable sin of attributing partners to Allah, while he may think he knows his Lord, since he knows himself.

The Way of Knowing Oneself and Knowing One's Lord

Then how is one to know oneself in order to know one's Lord?

The answer to this question is: Allah Most High exists and none other exists with Him. He is now as He has always been.

If one sees oneself as other than the only existence, which is Him, or if one does not see oneself as a part of Him, then the answer came from the Messenger of Allah when he said, "He who knows himself, knows his Lord." He did not mean by "self" one's ego—that self which favors the pleasures of the flesh and its lowly desires and which tries to command all of one; nor did he mean the self that first deceives—making one believe that the dirt and the ugliness is proper, then flagellates itself for the wrong it has done and forgets and does it again; nor did he mean the self-satisfied self. He meant one's truth, one's reality. When the Prophet (peace and blessings be upon him) prayed and said:

> O my lord, show me the reality of things

what he meant by "things" was those things that appear to be other than Allah. He meant, "Teach me those things other than You. What is all this around me? Let me know. These things—are they You, or are they other than You? Did they exist before or did they come to be? Are they here forever or are they going to pass away?"

And Allah showed him that the "things" had no being and He showed "them" to be Him, and it was seen that all that appeared as other than Allah was His being. He was shown things without a name, without time, without quality, as the essence of Allah.

The name of a thing is suggested by the thing to the one who names it, and by him is given to others. Thus, in a thing, the existence of the thing and the existence of its self are equivalent. Therefore, when the thing is known, the self is known and when the self is known the Lord is known.

You presume others to be other than Allah. There is nothing other than He, but you do not know this. While you are looking at Him you do not recognize Him. When the secret opens to you, you will know that you are none other than He. Then you will also know that you are the one whom he wished (but you need not disappear), and that you are forever and will not disappear with time, for there is no passing of time. Your attributes are His. Without a doubt, your appearance is His appearance. What is in you is in Him. Your before is His Before; your after is His After; your essence is His essence—without Him entering into you or you entering in Him, for

> Everything is perishing but His Face. (al-Qasas, 88)

That which exists and is visible is He. There is nothing but He, so how could nothing cease to be? There is only Him, His essence, which always will be. Therefore, if one knows that a thing exists that cannot cease to be, then the doubt and the ignorance about that thing will cease to be. That being is eternal, without changing into another being. When one who is sure of an existence joins with one who denies that existence, they do not unite. At best, the doubt about that existence disappears.

Therefore, do not think anymore that you need to become nothing, that you need to annihilate yourself in Him. If you thought so, then you would be His veil, while a veil over Allah is other than He. How could you be a veil that hides Him? What hides Him is His being the One Alone.

JUDAISM
The Essential Kabbalah

Daniel C. Matt

SINCE ITS APPEARANCE IN THE 12TH CENTURY, KABBALAH HAS BEEN AT the heart of Jewish mysticism. Traditionally communicated orally by a teacher or guide, Kabbalah reveals the direct knowledge of nonduality that Torah avoids but which was communicated to Moses and Adam by God.[1]

NONDUALITY

The essence of divinity is found in every single thing—nothing but it exists. Since it causes every thing to be, no thing can live by anything else. It enlivens them; its existence exists in each existent.

Do not attribute duality to God. Let God be solely God. If you suppose that Ein Sof emanates until a certain point, and that from that point on is outside of it, you have dualized. God forbid! Realize, rather, that Ein Sof exists in each existent. Do not say, "This is a stone and not God." God forbid! Rather, all existence is God, and the stone is a thing pervaded by divinity.

Before anything emanated, there was only Ein Sof. Ein Sof was all that existed. Similarly, after it brought into being that which exists, there is nothing but it. You cannot find anything that exists apart from it. There is nothing that is not pervaded by the power of divinity. God forbid! Rather, God is everything that exists, though everything that exists is not God. It is present in everything, and everything comes into being from it. Nothing is devoid of its divinity. Everything is within it; it is within everything and outside of everything. There is nothing but it.

God's Encampment

When you contemplate the Creator, realize that his encampment extends beyond, infinitely beyond, and so, too, in front of you and behind you, east and west, north and south, above and below, infinitely everywhere. Be aware that God fashioned everything and is within everything. There is nothing else.

The Chain of Being

God is unified oneness—one without two, inestimable. Genuine divine existence engenders the existence of all of creation. The sublime, inner essences secretly constitute a chain linking everything from the highest to the lowest, extending from the upper pool to the edge of the universe.

There is nothing—not even the tiniest thing—that is not fastened to the links of this chain. Everything is catenated in its mystery, caught in its oneness. God is one, God's secret is one, all the worlds below and above are all mysteriously one. Divine existence is indivisible.

The entire chain is one. Down to the last link, everything is linked with everything else; so divine essence is below as well as above, in heaven and on earth. There is nothing else.

EIN SOF AND YOU

Each of us emerges from Ein Sof and is included in it. We live through its dissemination. It is the perpetuation of existence. The fact that we sustain ourselves on vegetation and animal life does not mean that we are nourished on something outside of it. This process is like a revolving wheel, first descending, then ascending. It is all one and the same, nothing is separate from it. Though life branches out further and further, everything is joined to Ein Sof, included and abiding in it.

Delve into this. Flashes of intuition will come and go, and you will discover a secret here. If you are deserving, you will understand the mystery of God on your own.

YOU ENLIVEN EVERYTHING

There must be a contraction of God's presence. For if we believe that Ein Sof emanated the emanation and does not clothe itself within, then everything that emanated is outside of it, and it is outside of everything. Then there are two, God forbid. So we must conclude that nothing is outside of God. This applies not only to the sefirot but to everything that exists, large and small—they exist solely through the divine energy that flows to them and clothes itself in them. If God's gaze were withdrawn for even a moment, all existence would be nullified. This is the secret meaning of the verse: "You enliven everything." So divinity flows and inheres in each thing that exists. This is the secret meaning of the verse: "God's presence fills the entire world." Contemplating this, you are humbled, your thoughts are purified.

EIN SOF

Anything visible, and anything that can be grasped by thought, is bounded. Anything bounded is finite. Anything finite is not undifferentiated. Conversely, the boundless is called Ein Sof, Infinite. It is absolute undifferentiation in perfect, changeless oneness. Since it is boundless, there is nothing outside of it. Since it transcends and conceals itself, it is the essence of everything hidden and revealed. Since it is concealed, it is the root of faith and the root of rebellion. As it is written, "One who is righteous lives by his faith." The philosophers acknowledge that we comprehend it only by way of no.

Emanating from Ein Sof are the ten sefirot. They constitute the process by which all things come into being and pass away. They energize every existent thing that can be quantified. Since all things come into being by means of the sefirot, they differ from one another, yet they all derive from one root. Everything is from Ein Sof; there is nothing outside of it.

One should avoid fashioning metaphors regarding Ein Sof, but in order to help you understand, you can compare Ein Sof to a candle from which hundreds of millions of other candles are kindled. Though some shine brighter than others, compared to the first light they are all the same, all deriving from that one source. The first light and all the others are, in effect, incomparable. Nor can their priority compare with it, for it surpasses them; their energy emanates from it. No change takes place in it—the energy of emanation simply manifests through differentiation.

Ein Sof cannot be conceived, certainly not expressed, though it is intimated in every thing, for there is nothing outside of it. No letter, no name, no writing, no thing can confine it. The witness testifying in writing that there is nothing outside of it is, "I am that I am." Ein Sof has no will, no intention, no desire, no thought, no speech, no action—yet there is nothing outside of it.

THE AROMA OF INFINITY

Ein Sof does not abide being known, does not produce end or beginning.
Primordial Nothingness brought forth beginning and end.
Who is beginning?
The highest point, beginning of all, the concealed one abiding in thought.
It also engenders end, the culmination of the word.

But there, no end.
No desires, no lights, no sparks in that Infinity.
All these lights and sparks are dependent on it but cannot comprehend.
The only one who knows, yet without knowing, is the highest desire, concealed of all concealed,
Nothingness.
And when the highest point and the world that is coming ascend, they know only the aroma, as one inhaling an aroma is sweetened.

Oblivion

Ein Sof is a place to which forgetting and oblivion pertain. Why? Because concerning all the sefirot, one can search out their reality from the depth of supernal wisdom. From there it is possible to understand one thing from another. However, concerning Ein Sof, there is no aspect anywhere to search or probe; nothing can be known of it, for it is hidden and concealed in the mystery of absolute nothingness. Therefore forgetting pertains to the comprehension of this place. So open your eyes and see this great, awesome secret. Happy is one whose eyes shine from this secret, in this world and the world that is coming!

Ayin

Ayin, nothingness, is more existent than all the being of the world. But since it is simple, and every simple thing is complex compared with its simplicity, it is called Ayin.

The inner power is called Ayin because thought does not grasp it, nor reflection. Concerning this, Job said, "Wisdom comes into being out of ayin."

The Name of Nothingness

The depth of primordial being is called Boundless. Because of its concealment from all creatures above and below, it is also called Nothingness. If one asks, "What is it?" the answer is, "Nothing," meaning: No one can understand anything about it. It is negated of every conception. No one can know anything about it—except the belief that it exists. Its existence cannot be grasped by anyone other than it. Therefore its name is "I am becoming."

BEING AND NOTHINGNESS

You may be asked, "How did God bring forth being from nothingness? Is there not an immense difference between being and nothingness?"

Answer as follows: "Being is in nothingness in the mode of nothingness, and nothingness is in being in the mode of being." Nothingness is being and being is nothingness. The mode of being as it begins to emerge from nothingness into existence is called faith. For the term "faith" applies neither to visible, comprehensible being, nor to nothingness, invisible and incomprehensible, but rather to the nexus of nothingness and being. Being does not stem from nothingness alone but rather, from being and nothingness together. All is one in the simplicity of absolute undifferentiation. Our limited mind cannot grasp or fathom this, for it joins infinity.

THINK OF YOURSELF AS AYIN

Think of yourself as Ayin and forget yourself totally. Then you can transcend time, rising to the world of thought, where all is equal: life and death, ocean and dry land. Such is not the case if you are attached to the material nature of this world. If you think of yourself as something, then God cannot clothe himself in you, for God is infinite. No vessel can contain God, unless you think of yourself as Ayin.

THE ANNIHILATION OF THOUGHT

Thought rises to contemplate its own innerness until its power of comprehension is annihilated.

Taoism
The Tao Te Ching

Lao Tzu

THE VERSION QUOTED FROM HERE IS *Tao Te Ching: The Classic Book of Integrity and the Way,* translated by Victor H. Mair. It is based upon the Ma-wang-tui manuscripts, two silk manuscripts discovered in 1973 by Chinese archaeologists working at Ma-wang-tui located "in central China about a hundred miles south of the Yangtze river."

Introduction by Victor H. Mair

Next to the Bible and the *Bhagavad Gita*, the *Tao Te Ching* is the most translated book in the world. Well over a hundred different renditions of the Taoist classic have been made into English alone, not to mention the dozens in German, French, Italian, Dutch, Latin, and other European languages. There are several reasons for the superabundance of translations. The first is that the *Tao Te Ching* is considered to be the fundamental text of both philosophical and religious Taoism. Indeed, the Tao, or Way, which is at the heart of the *Tao Te Ching*, is also the centerpiece of all Chinese religion and thought. Naturally, different schools and sects bring somewhat different slants to the Tao, but all subscribe to the notion that there is a single, overarching Way that encompasses everything in the universe. As such, the *Tao Te Ching* shares crucial points of similarity with other major religious scriptures the world over.

The second reason for the popularity of the *Tao Te Ching* is its brevity. There are few bona fide classics that are so short, yet so packed with food for thought. One can read and reread the *Tao Te Ching* scores of times without exhausting the insights it offers.

The third aspect that accounts for the wide repute of the *Tao Te Ching* is its deceptive simplicity: In the words of the author himself, it is supposedly "very easy to understand," when actually it is quite difficult to comprehend fully. Paradox is the essence of the *Tao Te Ching*, so much so that even scholars with a solid grounding in classical Chinese cannot be sure they have grasped what the Old Master is really saying in his pithy maxims. For this reason, I vowed two decades ago that I would never attempt to translate the *Tao Te Ching*. However, an unexpected event forced me to recant: The recent discovery of two ancient manuscripts in China made it possible to produce a totally new translation of the *Tao Te Ching* far more accurate and reliable than any published previously. These manuscripts are at least a half millennium older than commonly translated versions.

This translation of the *Tao Te Ching* is based wholly on these new-found manuscripts. Their availability has made it possible to strip away the distortions and obfuscations of a tradition that has striven for two millennia to "improve" the text with commentaries and interpretations more amenable to various religious, philosophical, and political persuasions. And they have provided me with the means to make the translation in this book significantly different from all other previously existing translations.

SELECTIONS FROM THE TAO TE CHING

The translator provides a note regarding the numbering of the chapters: "The numbers running consecutively from 1 to 81 follow the sequence of the Ma-wang-tui manuscripts. The numbers in parentheses indicate the corresponding chapters of the previous standard text."

1 (38)

The person of superior integrity
does not insist upon his integrity;
For this reason, he has integrity.
The person of inferior integrity
never loses sight of his integrity;
For this reason, he lacks integrity.

The person of superior integrity takes no action,
nor has he a purpose for acting
The person of superior humaneness takes action,
but has no purpose for acting.
The person of superior righteousness takes action,
and has a purpose for acting.
The person of superior etiquette takes action,
but others do not respond to him;
Whereupon he rolls up his sleeves
and coerces them.

Therefore,
When the Way is lost,
afterward comes integrity.
When integrity is lost,
afterward comes humaneness.
When humaneness is lost,

afterward comes righteousness.
When righteousness is lost,
afterward comes etiquette.

Now,
Etiquette is the attenuation of trustworthiness,
and the source of disorder.
Foreknowledge is but the blossomy ornament of the Way,
and the source of ignorance.

For this reason,
The great man resides in substance,
not in attenuation.
He resides in fruitful reality,
not in blossomy ornament.
Therefore,
He rejects the one and adopts the other.

6 (43)

The softest thing under heaven
gallops triumphantly over
The hardest thing under heaven.

Nonbeing penetrates nonspace,
Hence,
I know the advantages of nonaction.

The doctrine without words,
The advantage of nonaction—
few under heaven can realize these!

12 (49)

The sage never has a mind of his own;
He considers the minds of the common people to be his mind.

Treat well those who are good,
Also treat well those who are not good;
thus is goodness attained.

Be sincere to those who are sincere,
Also be sincere to those who are insincere;
thus is sincerity attained.

The sage
is self-effacing in his dealings with all under heaven,
and bemuddles his mind for the sake of all under heaven.

The common people all rivet their eyes and ears upon him,
And the sage makes them all chuckle like children.

36 (71)

To realize that you do not understand is a virtue;
Not to realize that you do not understand is a defect.

The reason why
The sage has no defects,
Is because he treats defects as defects.

Thus,
He has no defects.

45 (1)

The ways that can be walked are not the eternal Way;
The names that can be named are not the eternal name.
The nameless is the origin of the myriad creatures;
The named is the mother of the myriad creatures.

Therefore,
Always be without desire

in order to observe its wondrous subtleties;
Always have desire
so that you may observe its manifestations.

Both of these derive from the same source;
They have different names but the same designation.

Mystery of mysteries,
The gate of all wonders!

55 (11)

Thirty spokes converge on a single hub,
but it is in the space where there is nothing
that the usefulness of the cart lies.
Clay is molded to make a pot,
but it is in the space where there is nothing
that the usefulness of the clay pot lies.
Cut out doors and windows to make a room,
but it is in the spaces where there is nothing
that the usefulness of the room lies.

Therefore,
Benefit may be derived from something,
but it is in nothing that we find usefulness.

63 (19)

"Abolish sagehood and abandon cunning,
the people will benefit a hundredfold;
Abolish humaneness and abandon righteousness,
the people will once again be filial and kind;
Abolish cleverness and abandon profit,
bandits and thieves will be no more."

These three statements
are inadequate as a civilizing doctrine;
Therefore,
Let something be added to them:

Evince the plainness of undyed silk,
Embrace the simplicity of the unhewn log;
Lessen selfishness,
Diminish desires;
Abolish learning
and you will be without worries.

Native American Tradition
The Ways of the Spirit

Ohiyesa

Introduction by Kent Nerburn

Unlike many traditions, the spiritual wisdom of the Native Americans is not found in a set of "scriptural" materials. It is, and always has been, a part of the fabric of daily life and experience.

One of the most fascinating and overlooked individuals in American history (is) Ohiyesa, also known by the Anglicized name of Charles Alexander Eastman.

Ohiyesa was, at heart, a poet of the spirit and the bearer of spiritual wisdom. To the extent that he dared, and with increasing fervor as he aged, he was a preacher for the native vision of life. It is my considered belief it is his spiritual vision, above all else, that we of our generation need to hear. We hunger for the words and insights of the Native American, and no man spoke with more clarity than Ohiyesa.

Ohiyesa was born in southern Minnesota in the area now called Redwood Falls in the winter of 1858. He was a member of the Dakota, Sioux, nation. When he was four, his people rose up in desperation against the U.S. Government, which was systematically starving them by withholding provisions and payment they were owed from the sale of their land.

When their uprising was crushed, more than a thousand men, women, and children were captured and taken away. On the day after Christmas in 1862, thirty-eight of the men were hanged at Mankato, Minnesota, in the greatest mass execution ever performed by the U.S. Government. Those who were not killed were taken to stockades and holding camps, where they faced starvation and death during the icy days of northern winter.

Ohiyesa's father, Many Lightnings, was among those captured.

Ohiyesa, who was among those left behind, was handed over to his uncle to be raised in the traditional Sioux manner. He was taught the ways of the forest and lessons of his people. He strove to become a hunter and a warrior. Then, one day while he was hunting, he saw an Indian walking toward him in white man's clothes. It was his father, who had survived the internment camps and had returned to claim his son.

During his incarceration, Many Lightnings had seen the power of the European culture and had become convinced that the Indian way of life could not survive within it. He despised what he called "reservation Indians" who gave up their independence and tradition in order to accept a handout from the European conquerors.

He took Ohiyesa to a small plot of farming land in eastern South Dakota and began teaching him to be a new type of warrior. He sent him off to white schools with the admonition that "it is the same as if I sent you on your first warpath. I shall expect you to conquer."

Thus was born Charles Alexander Eastman, the Santee Sioux child of the woodlands and prairies who would go on to become the adviser to presidents and an honored member of New England society.

Ohiyesa, or Eastman, went to Beloit College where he learned English and immersed himself in the culture and ways of the white world. Upon graduation he went east. He attended Dartmouth College, then was accepted into medical school at Boston University, which he completed in 1890. He returned to his native Midwest to work among his own people as a physician on the Pine Ridge reservation, but became disenchanted with the corruption of the U.S. Government and its Indian agents. After a short-lived effort to establish a private medical practice in St. Paul, Minnesota, he turned his focus back to the issue of Indian-white relations.

For the next twenty-five years, he was involved in various efforts to build bridges of understanding between Indians and non-Indian people of America. He worked first for the YMCA, then served as an attorney for his people in Washington, then returned to South Dakota to spend three years as physician for the Sioux at Crow Creek.

In 1903 he went back to Massachusetts and devoted himself to bringing the voice of the Indian into the American intellectual arena. He became deeply involved in the Boy Scout program, believing it was the best way to give non-Indian American youth a sense of the wonder and values that he had learned growing up in the wild.

Eventually, with the help of his wife, he established a camp of his own in New Hampshire in which he tried to recreate the experience of Sioux education and values for non-Indian children.

But financial troubles and the fundamentally irreconcilable differences between Indian culture and white civilization ultimately took their toll. In 1918 he and his white wife separated, and in 1921 he left New England for good. He continued to believe that the way of civilization was the way of the future, but he had lost much of his faith in its capacity to speak to the higher moral and spiritual vision of humanity. He returned again to his native forests of the Midwest, devoting more time to his traditional ways, often going into the woods alone for months at a time.

But he never ceased believing that the two cultures that had clashed so tragically on the soil of the American continent somehow had to become one if there ever was to be a true America with an honest and indigenous soul. Even though he had come to believe that white civilization was, at heart, "a system of life based on trade," he still felt that it was the task of the best people, both Indian and non-Indian, to help America find a shared vision. As he said at the end of his autobiography, *From Deep Woods to Civilization*, "I am an Indian; and while I have learned much from civilization, for which I am grateful, I have never lost my Indian sense of right and justice. I am for development and progress along social and spiritual lines, rather than those of commerce, nationalism, or efficiency. Nevertheless, so long as I live, I am an American."

As an observer of Indian life, Ohiyesa was unlike any other. He was at once completely secure in his Indian identity, yet gave himself over completely to the search for meaning within the context of a European America. He tried with his whole heart and spirit to believe in the wisdom of each of the ways he had learned. If there was a struggle, it was because the two ways coexisted so uneasily within one person.

Though he lamented the passing of the Indian ways, he accepted it as the workings of the Great Mystery, and set himself to the dual task of bringing the ways of the whites to the Indians and the ways of the Indians to the whites. He never lost his grounding in his traditional ways, even while exploring the intricacies of "the Christ Ideal" and dining with presidents. He was ever the observer, journeying ever deeper into the ways of white culture, trying, as his grandmother had always instructed him, "to follow a new trail to the point of knowing."

The writings he has left are the documents of that journey, crafted by a man with a warrior's heart, an orator's tongue, and human spirit of such dignity that it transcends boundaries of race and belief. A selection from these writings follows.

THE WAYS OF THE SPIRIT

Is there not something worthy of perpetuation in our Indian spirit of democracy, where Earth, our mother, was free to all, and no one sought to impoverish or enslave his neighbor?

The Great Mystery

The attitude of the American Indian toward the Eternal, the Great Mystery that surrounds and embraces us, is as simple as it is exalted. To us it is the supreme conception, bringing with it the fullest measure of joy and satisfaction possible in this life.

The worship of the Great Mystery is silent, solitary, free from all self-seeking.

It is silent, because all speech is of necessity feeble and imperfect; therefore the souls of our ancestor ascended to God in wordless adoration.

It is solitary, because we believe that God is nearer to us in solitude, and there are no priests authorized to come between us and our Maker. None can exhort or confess or in any way meddle with the religious experience of another. All of us are created children of God, and all stand erect, conscious of our divinity. Our faith cannot be formulated in creeds, nor forced upon any who are unwilling to receive it; hence there is no preaching, proselytizing, nor persecution, neither are there any scoffers or atheists.

Our religion is an attitude of mind, not a dogma.

The Temple of Nature

There are no temples or shrines among us save those of nature. Being children of nature, we are intensely poetical. We would deem it sacrilege to build a house for The One who may be met face to face in the mysterious, shadowy aisles of the primeval forest, or on the sunlit bosom of virgin prairies, upon dizzy spires and pinnacles of naked rock, and in the vast jeweled vault of the night sky! A God who is enrobed in filmy veils of cloud, there on the rim of the visible world where our Great-Grandfather Sun kindles his evening camp-fire; who rides upon the rigorous wind of the north, or breathes forth spirit upon fragrant southern airs, whose war canoe is launched upon majestic rivers and inland seas—such a God needs no lesser cathedral.

The Power of Silence

We first Americans mingle with our pride an exceptional humility. Spiritual arrogance is foreign to our nature and teaching. We never claimed that the power of articulate speech is proof of superiority over "dumb creation;" on the other hand, it is to us a perilous gift.

We believe profoundly in silence—the sign of a perfect equilibrium. Silence is the absolute poise or balance of body, mind, and spirit. Those who can preserve their selfhood ever calm and unshaken by the storms of existence—not a leaf, as it were, astir on the tree; not a ripple upon the shining pool—those, in the mind of the person of nature, possess the ideal attitude and conduct of life.

If you ask us, "What is silence?" we will answer, "It is the Great Mystery. The holy silence is God's voice."

If you ask, "What are the fruits of silence?" we will answer, "They are self-control, true courage or endurance, patience, dignity, and reverence. Silence is the cornerstone of character."

"Guard your tongue in youth," said the old chief, Wabasha, "and in age you may mature a thought that will be service to your people."

The Power of Spirit

Naturally magnanimous and open-minded, we have always preferred to believe that the Spirit of God is not breathed into humans alone, but that the whole created universe shares in the immortal perfection of its Maker.

The elements and majestic forces in nature—lightning, wind, water, fire, and frost—are regarded with awe as spiritual powers, but always secondary and intermediate in character. We believe that the spirit pervades all creation and that every creature possesses a soul in some degree, though not necessarily a soul conscious of itself. The tree, the waterfall, the grizzly bear, each is an embodied Force, and as such an object of reverence.

We Indians love to come into sympathy and spiritual communion with our brothers and sisters of the animal kingdom, whose inarticulate souls hold for us something of the sinless purity that we attribute to the innocent and irresponsible child. We have a faith in their instincts, as in a mysterious wisdom given from above; and while we humbly accept the sacrifice of their bodies to preserve our own, we pay homage to their spirits in prescribed prayers and offerings.

Poverty and Simplicity

We original Americans have generally been despised by our conquerors for our poverty and simplicity. They forget, perhaps, that our religion forbade the accumulation of wealth and the enjoyment of luxury. To us, as to other spiritually-minded people in every age and race, the love of possessions is a snare, and the burdens of a complex society a source of needless peril and temptation.

It is the simple truth that we Indians did not, so long as our native philosophy held sway over our minds, either envy or desire to imitate the splendid achievements of the white race. In our own thought we rose superior to them! We scorned them, even as a lofty spirit absorbed in its own task rejects the soft beds, the luxurious food, the pleasure-worshipping dalliance of a rich neighbor. It was clear to us that virtue and happiness are independent of these things, if not incompatible with them.

Furthermore, it was the rule of our life to share the fruits of our skill and success with our less fortunate brothers and sisters. Thus we kept our spirits free from the clog of pride, avarice, or envy, and carried out, as we believed, the divine decree—a matter profoundly important to us.

Nature and Solitude

As children of nature, we have always looked upon the concentration of population as the prolific mother of all evils, moral no less than physical. It was not, then, wholly from ignorance or improvidence that we failed to establish permanent towns and to develop a material civilization. We have always believed that food is good, while surfeit kills; that love is good, but lust destroys; and not less dreaded than the pestilence following upon crowded and unsanitary dwellings is the loss of spiritual power inseparable from too close contact with one's fellow men.

All who have lived much out of doors, whether Indian or otherwise, know that there is a magnetic and powerful force that accumulates in solitude but is quickly dissipated by life in a crowd. Even our enemies have recognized that for a certain innate power and self-poise, wholly independent of circumstances, the American Indian is unsurpassed among the races.

The Importance of Prayer

Prayer—the daily recognition of the Unseen and the Eternal—is our one inevitable duty.

We Indian people have traditionally divided mind into two parts—the spiritual mind and the physical mind. The first—the spiritual mind—is concerned only with the essence of things, and it is this we seek to strengthen by spiritual prayer, during which the body is subdued by fasting and hardship. In this type of prayer there is no beseeching of favor or help.

The second, or physical, mind, is lower. It is concerned with all personal or selfish matters, like success in hunting or warfare, relief from sickness, or the sparing of a beloved life. All ceremonies, charms, or incantations designed to secure a benefit or to avert a danger are recognized as emanating from the physical self.

The rites of this physical worship are wholly symbolic; we may have sundances and other ceremonies, but the Indian no more worships the sun than the Christian worships the cross. In our view, the Sun and the Earth are the parents of all organic life. And, it must be admitted, in this our thinking is scientific truth as well as poetic metaphor.

For the Sun, as the universal father, sparks the principle of growth in nature, and in the patient and fruitful womb of our mother, the

Earth, are hidden embryos of plants and men. Therefore our reverence and love for the Sun and the Earth are really an imaginative extension of our love for our immediate parents, and with this feeling of filial devotion is joined a willingness to appeal to them for such good gifts as we may desire. This is the material or physical prayer.

But, in a broader sense, our whole life is prayer because every act of our life is, in a very real sense, a religious act. Our daily devotions are more important to us than food.

We wake at daybreak, put on our moccasins and step down to the water's edge. Here we throw handfuls of clear, cold water into our face, or plunge in bodily.

After the bath, we stand erect before the advancing dawn, facing the sun as it dances upon the horizon, and offer our unspoken prayer. Our mate may proceed or follow us in our devotions, but never accompanies us. Each soul must meet the morning sun, the new sweet earth, and the Great Silence alone.

Whenever, in the course of our day, we might come upon a scene that is strikingly beautiful or sublime—the black thundercloud with the rainbow's glowing arch above the mountain; a white waterfall in the heart of a green gorge; a vast prairie tinged with the blood-red sunset—we pause for an instant in the attitude of worship.

We recognize the spirit in all creation, and believe that we draw spiritual power from it. Our respect for the immortal part of our brothers and sisters, the animals, often leads us so far as to lay out the body of any game we catch and decorate the head with symbolic paint or feathers. We then stand before it in an attitude of prayer, holding up the pipe that contains our sacred tobacco, as a gesture that we have freed with honor the spirit of our brother or sister, whose body we were compelled to take to sustain our own life.

When food is taken, the woman murmurs a "grace"—an act so softly and unobtrusively performed that one who does not know the custom usually fails to catch the whisper: "Spirit, partake!"

As her husband receives his bowl or plate, he likewise murmurs his invocation to the spirit. When he becomes an old man, he loves to make a particular effort to prove his gratitude. He cuts off the choicest morsel of the meat and casts it into the fire—the purest and most ethereal element.

Thus we see no need for the setting apart one day in seven as a holy day, since to us all days belong to God.

The Appreciation of Beauty

In the appreciation of beauty, which is closely akin to religious feeling, the American Indian stands alone. In accord with our nature and beliefs, we do not pretend to imitate the inimitable, or to reproduce exactly the work of the Great Artist. That which is beautiful must not be trafficked with, but must only be revered and adored.

I have seen in our midsummer celebrations cool arbors built of fresh-cut branches for council and dance halls, while those who attended decked themselves with leafy boughs, carrying shields and fans of the same, and even making wreaths for their horses' necks. But, strange to say, they seldom make free use of flowers. I once asked the reason for this.

"Why," said one, "the flowers are for our souls to enjoy; not for our bodies to wear. Leave them alone and they will live out their lives and reproduce themselves as the Great Gardener intended. He planted them; we must not pluck them, for it would be selfish to do so."

This is the spirit of the original American. We hold nature to be the measure of consummate beauty, and we consider its destruction to be a sacrilege.

I once showed a party of Sioux chiefs the sights of Washington, and endeavored to impress them with the wonderful achievements of civilization. After visiting the Capitol and other famous buildings, we passed through the Corcoran Art Gallery, where I tried to explain how the white man valued this or that painting as a work of genius and a masterpiece of art.

"Ah!" exclaimed an old man, "such is the strange philosophy of the white man! He hews down the forest that has stood for centuries in its pride and grandeur, tears up the bosom of Mother Earth, and causes the silvery watercourses to waste and vanish away.

He ruthlessly disfigures God's own pictures and monuments, and then daubs a flat surface with many colors, and praises his work as a masterpiece!"

Here we have the root of the failure of the Indian to approach the "artistic" standard of the civilized world. It lies not in our lack of creative imagination—for in this quality we are born artists—it lies rather in our point of view. Beauty, in our eyes, is always fresh and living, even as God, the Great Mystery, dresses the world anew at each season of the year.

The Miracle of the Ordinary

We Indians have always been clear thinkers within the scope of our understanding, but cause and effect have not formed the basis for our thinking. We do not chart and measure the vast field of nature or express her wonders in the terms of science; on the contrary, we see miracles on every hand—the miracle of life in seed and egg, the miracle of death in a lightning flash and in the swelling deep!

Nothing of the marvelous can astonish us—a beast could speak or the sun stand still. The virgin birth seems scarcely more miraculous than is the birth of every child that comes into the world, and the miracle of the loaves and fishes excites no greater wonder than the harvest that springs from a single ear of corn.

Let us not forget that even for the most contemporary thinker, who sees a majesty and grandeur in natural law, science cannot explain everything. We all still have to face the ultimate miracle—the origin and principle of life. This is the supreme mystery that is the essence of worship and without which there can be no religion. In the presence of this mystery all peoples must take an attitude much like that of the Indian, who beholds with awe the Divine in all creation.

CHRISTIANITY
Steps in My Christian Passage

Bernadette Roberts

THE DIVINE OR TRINITARIAN CHRIST IS ETERNAL FORM. THIS FORM, however, is not what the ordinary senses see as form, or what the mind knows as form (including Platonic form or an idea in the divine mind), or what consciousness experiences as form. Rather, Eternal Form is concrete, material, physical, the underlying substance of all matter. Without it there would be no universe and no one to see it. So Eternal Form is not apart from what we see, yet it is also not what we see. In order to come upon Eternal Form, all form must first be an absolute void where nothing can possibly be relative to it; it is only from this position that Eternal Form can be revealed.

By definition the divine or Absolute is "that" which is nonrelative, and the only thing that can be nonrelative is a void of voids. This void of voids or absolute nothing IS Christ.

What I inappropriately called the "smile of recognition"[1] is also what I call "the resurrection." This is because it is the recognition of the true nature of the body or "that" which remains beyond all self. The ultimate nature of the body is Eternal Form or Christ; it is the true nature of the divine Manifest or Trinitarian Christ. Form and the Formless, Father and Christ, are one from all eternity. We say God made all things from nothing or that all things arose from the void of voids, but this nothing or void IS Eternal Form or Christ. In other words, whatever we are made of—we do not know its essence, which is forever beyond the scientific mind—IS Christ. The resurrection, then, is the revelation of the true nature of the body, its eternal nature. The body (and all form) is Eternal Form; it is the divine Christ and all that is manifest of the unmanifest Father. The unmanifest void (Father) is not Eternal Form (Christ); at the same time neither are they separate. As One they constitute the eternal Godhead of the Trinity.

As I know it, then, the true nature of Christ's death is the falling away of self or consciousness, followed by the "descent into hell," the void of voids. From this void Christ rises to reveal the divine nature of the body, Eternal Form or mystical body of God. It is not just Christ's single historical body that is revealed, but the ultimate nature of all bodies or form. Eternal Form is the All and Everywhere of the divine, which means we cannot point to any single form and say "There is the divine," or point to any person and say "He or she is the divine," nor can we refer to any experience and say "This is the divine." Even when we point to the historical Christ we cannot point to his divinity, only to his humanity. Consciousness had been responsible for experientially focusing on God or pinpointing the divine as this or that experience or individual. But beyond consciousness God as Eternal Form is Everywhere, neither the singular (he, she or it) nor the multiple (an additive of "all together"), but rather One Absolute Eternal Form. This is Christ, the eternal Form of the Formless.

The truth of the body, then, is the revelation that Christ is all that is manifest of God or all that is manifest of the unmanifest Father. Self or consciousness does not reveal this and cannot know it. In the "smile" there was no knower or one who smiles, nor was there anyone or anything to smile at or to know; there was just the smile, the "knowing" that is beyond knower and known. The wrong interpretation of the absence of knower and known is that in the Godhead knower and known are identical. But the identity of knower and known is only true of consciousness, which is self knowing itself. But the Godhead transcends this identity—it is void of knower or known. The "knowing" that remains beyond self or consciousness cannot be accounted for in any terms of knower or known. The truest thing that could be said is that the "body knows."

After the smile of recognition, the void of voids lifted and was never encountered again. By this time it was almost eighteen months after the initial falling away of self. Altogether, however, it took two to three years to finally acclimate to the no-self condition or dimension of living. This acclimation consists of the senses having to stay awake and remain functional without any self or consciousness. The tendency was for the senses to continually fall into the Great Silence—close down or drop out—which would have resulted in death. At one point in particular, this was indeed an imminent possibility. Without consciousness or the senses, all that is left is the vegetative body, which, without man-made (not God-made) support, moves into the divine. For the senses to stay awake without consciousness is so enormously difficult that I know without doubt that this resurrected condition is not meant for this world. The resurrected state is not the true human condition, nor is it man's final estate. While the unitive state is indeed man's true mature state in this world, the no-self condition is not compatible or even integrable with the human condition. That which was integrable—self or consciousness—is gone. The resurrected condition is incapable of true involvement in this world; as said before, its sole purpose is to affirm ultimate Truth. In Christ's case the resurrection revealed Truth, but for those who follow, the resurrection affirms Christ's Truth—a Truth that every human being will come upon some day.

About six months after the above events, I wrote *The Experience of No-Self* and basically considered the journey finished. At this point it never occurred to me that there was more down the road or that there was yet more to Christ's revelation. But after another year or so—perhaps three or four years after the falling away of self—there occurred a further disclosure of Christ.

ASCENSION

After communion one morning the body seemingly began to inhale (though it did not come from the outside) what I can only describe as a type of odorless anesthetic (reminiscent of ether) that instantly spread from the lungs to the entire body. It was as if every atom or cell of the body had given way or was disclosed as a kind of elemental gas or "divine air." While there is no possible description for this divine air, it would not be entirely improper (based on the experience alone) to affirm that "God is a gas." It was as if every cell or element of which the body was composed WAS this "divine air," and that every element of the body dwelled in this indescribably divine and glorious state of existence. It was as if the body had dissolved into this "divine air," or better put, that the true body (Eternal Form or Christ's mystical body) dwelled eternally in this glorious divine estate. A few seconds into this phenomenon of the body dissolving into "divine air," there was instant recognition of the ascension experience. No mind, intellect or self is needed for this recognition; all that is needed is a physical body. We might compare this knowing to the mysterious "wisdom of the body" that we take so lightly throughout our lives, a wisdom beyond all self or consciousness. This condition, however, is incompatible with continued sensory existence or bodily functioning. Like an anesthetic, it closes down the senses; at one point the air became so heavy and condensed that continued breathing was all but impossible. If, at this moment, the air had not thinned, there would be no body remaining to give this account.

As for a description of this "divine air" no word enters the mind; it simply puts an end to the mind. About all that can be said is that if we put together man's loftiest experiences of ecstasy, bliss, love and all things ineffable, they fall as short of the divine condition as the size of an ant falls short of that of an elephant. Consciousness' most lofty heavenly experiences of the divine are but a palest shadow of the ultimate divine condition or "heaven." While I do not like calling this heavenly estate a "condition," I do so to differentiate it from a passing state or stage as well as from "experience," which is always and everywhere a temporary non-eternal phenomenon. The final estate has no description because it never reaches the mind—"eye hath not seen nor the ear heard, nor has it ever entered into the mind of man." Heaven or "the kingdom of God is not of this world."

Because consciousness or the mind cannot form any notion of the ascension, I wish to make clear that this particular experience is not a dissolving or disappearance of the body; it is not an out-of-the-body experience or the experience of a soul leaving the body. It was not an experience of bodilessness or the discovery of some other body and so on. Rather, it is the clear disclosure that the unknown substance of the physical body (Eternal Form or Christ's mystical body) dwells in a divine (heavenly or glorious) condition, which condition IS the unmanifest divine or Father. Thus where the resurrection reveals Christ as Eternal Form, the ascension reveals the unmanifest or Formless Father as the glorious condition in which Eternal Form dwells or exists. In itself a heavenly condition cannot be manifest, concretized or materialized; for this reason it always remains unmanifest. But the unmanifest is not all there IS to the divine; rather the unmanifest is eternally one with the manifest, which is why we say Christ is all that is manifest of the unmanifest. Too often we think that Christ was only "manifest" at the time of the incarnation, but the incarnation was only the revelation of the manifest divine. The divine manifest Christ is from all eternity; the incarnation was only the revelation of this Truth to man.

The historical Christ never verbalized this great Truth (which nobody would have understood anyway), but silently demonstrated it with his resurrection and ascension. As we know, Christ's body dissolved into air, became invisible to the mind and senses, but what is this "air" into which Christ disappeared? This "air" is not only

Christ's Eternal Form but the unmanifest condition (the Father) in which this Form eternally dwells. Like the resurrection the ascension reveals the inseparability of spirit and matter, the Formless and Form, which means that what man or consciousness does not know about spirit IS matter, and what he does not know about matter IS spirit; one is the mystery of the other.

This ascension experience was not a mere passing glimpse of truth. For about six weeks the divine air varied in intensity just enough to allow a minimum of mundane existence. On one occasion, at a point of highest intensity, it seemed that the senses were going to permanently "drop" away—the expression "drop" describes a particular physical sensation that accompanied the falling away of consciousness and will accompany the eventual falling away of the senses. I can only compare this situation to having both feet in heaven, but without the door of earthly existence permanently closing behind us. After this there was a gradually lessening of the "divine air" and the senses slowly came back to their more ordinary functioning—their functioning in the resurrected condition, that is.

INCARNATION

The next disclosure followed as a result of the ascension experience. With the lessening of the "divine air" (the unmanifest's divine condition) there was a gradual return to the former resurrected state. This return was a reversal of the ascension experience. Where the ascension had been a dissolution into the divine, here now, there was a coming out of the divine and a readjustment to full sensory perception (staying wide awake to the world, that is) which took between six and nine months. This was actually the second time there had to be an acclimation to the resurrected state; only this time, from a different side of the resurrection. Where the first adjustment followed the falling away of self, the second adjustment is the return from the ascension with its near falling away of the senses. Anything I can say about this return or adjustment is but a shadow of its reality; let me just say that it was so difficult and terrible that, in comparison, the void of voids was easy going.

Having to leave the divine condition and come back to the sensory or resurrected state can only be described as GOD-AWFUL; it is an inhuman predicament, even an inhuman feat. This is more, however, than just a return to a previous state; it was a waking up to a sensory terrain and human condition that, compared to the divine condition, could only be described as "hell." (It was not even a living hell because none of it was seen as true life.) In contrast to the divine, the human condition is so terrible and devastating that even the worst of descriptions could never do it justice. I am not referring here to sin, evil or suffering, but rather to bare human existence itself—and the whole natural world included. What we usually think is so beautiful in this world is actually monstrous and unbearable to look at, but only in contrast to the divine.

Compared to this ordeal of entering the human condition, all our notions and experiences of suffering are as nothing. It was as if the divine were undergoing a terrible ordeal trying to stay awake to this world without falling back into the divine condition—because this world was so ugly and void. Again it was as if the divine were going against itself and its own nature because of its determined will to be in this world as a human being. Despite this terrible predicament, there was about this acclimation a knowledge that a mysterious divine feat was taking place. At one point I understood that this reversal of the ascension experience was not like any other return; rather, this coming down or out of the divine was akin to the "incarnation experience."

No one can understand this particular view of the world and the human condition unless he has first known the ultimate divine estate (heaven) and then returned (or originally come out of it as in the case of the incarnate Christ) to this world's condition. Those who believe man can have both heaven and this world at the same time are very much mistaken; such a notion is a total underestimation of God's utter transcendence, as well as heaven or man's final estate. Compared to the divine estate there is no beauty or happiness in this world; thus man cannot afford to have a glimpse or taste of the final estate and still expect to find this world acceptable. The ultimate estate is not of this world; it is not even compatible with it—which is why there is death. For this reason it is good that man does not see the reality of the divine beyond consciousness, for if he did he could not endure this world. What man does not know, he does not miss, and what he does not know is how utterly transcendent the divine really is. Thus man can settle for the world and the divine he knows, because this is all he knows. This is the way things were made to be. God fashioned consciousness, which is why it has no place else to go, or comes to no other end than in the divine.

Where full acclimation to the resurrected state had been difficult, after the ascension it seemed impossible. Until this point the journey had been an irreversible forward movement, but here the movement had reversed itself. Thus for God to take on consciousness it was necessary to forfeit the ultimate beatific condition, since to dwell in both conditions (beatific and human) at the same time is impossible. In moving from the divine to the human condition, Christ had to undergo the GOD-AWFUL forfeiture of the ultimate divine condition in order to take on consciousness directly from the divine condition. Man never goes through this GOD-AWFUL experience when coming into this world. Man comes from the manifest, the void of voids or out of darkness, whereas the incarnate Christ came from the unmanifest (divine heavenly condition) or out of Light and into our darkness.

So the movement of the incarnation is this: Christ moves down from the ultimate divine condition into the ascension experience; from here he moves down to the resurrected condition (sensory); and from here he moves further down into consciousness and into the unitive or egoless state in which he was born. Thus Christ came down the way man goes up; they are reverse passages. At his birth, however, Christ begins his return home, and in the return takes all men with him. We generally think of the revelation of Truth as a marvelous thing, but what no one realizes is that ultimate Truth is basically unbearable to man—to the senses, the mind, consciousness, the whole body in fact. In the end the fullness of Truth is virtually the death of man. Solely on an intellectual level, when man comes upon this Truth he usually takes it for an error. He does so out of ignorance because final Truth is unbelievable. This is why naked faith is the only way to make the passage.

Although the incarnation experience is devastating in its GOD-AWFULNESS, nowhere else in the journey is the Reality and Truth of Christ more obvious or absolute than in this ordeal. It should be remembered, however, this world is only GOD-AWFUL for someone who is not of this world or who is coming into this world directly from the divine condition. It is the sheer contrast between the divine condition and the purely sensory or resurrected state that is responsible for the GOD-AWFULNESS of the incarnation experience. No human being could ever see the world or human existence this way; in fact, even God does not ordinarily see it this way. It is only in the incarnation when the divine takes on the human condition and has to forego or preclude the divine condition that the divine undergoes such a terrible ordeal. For this reason I regard the incarnation as Christ's true "saving" act; compared to this his death is a blessed release, a glorious ascent back to his divine condition.

Altogether it took about nine months to fully acclimate once again to the resurrected condition. But after the experience of ascension and incarnation, the resurrected state was altered; it was not the same as before. The only way it is the same is that it is livable, and for all practical purposes this is probably all that matters. It is different because, having come upon the final divine estate, there can never again be any real acclimation to this world. By itself the resurrected state is enough to preclude this possibility, but after the ascension it is forever impossible. All that is left now is the Eucharist; everything else is sheer burden. While I regard the initial no-self condition as the resurrected state, after the ascension and incarnation, what remains is only the "Eucharistic state." Eucharist is the final word on Christ.

IN THE END

As someone who began the journey as a child not honestly able to believe that Christ was God, this journey went beyond anything I ever thought possible—and not only for myself, but above all for

Christ. I never suspected the extent of his mystery or Truth. Evidently this Truth had to be learned the hard way because I was never able to believe in the same manner that many other people are privileged to believe. The one thing I can say, however, is that everything I know of Christ is solely through living experience. It did not come by way of intellectual belief, concepts, symbols, or passing insights. Although it was a very prolonged and difficult journey, it was all within ordinary daily living and not due to any extraordinary circumstance, opportunity or position in life. What was extraordinary was not the person or the life, but the grace; it more than stretched the human limits.

But what was this journey all about? Well, I only have one view of it, the only view I can really have—it was a gradual revelation of the truth of Christ. The revelation of God, the divine or Absolute, never provided the challenge or mystery that kept the journey going; if my only concern had been the experience of the Absolute, the journey could have been over before it had begun. But Christ is a further revelation of the Absolute, a revelation that challenges us to penetrate not only the nature of the Absolute, but our human nature as well. Although every Christian is on a journey, as to why there are different journeys within a single tradition I can only say that it may have to do with different levels of belief or faith. Though I did not start from disbelief or a refusal to believe, I had to start from no-belief or the inability to believe, and perhaps this was why my journey was so difficult. Christ said, "Blessed are those who believe and do not see." Obviously I was not one of those so blessed. Yet even without believing I did eventually see. And what this means to me is that in the end, whether man believes in Christ or not, he WILL SEE. This I know absolutely.

After the seeing or realization I call the resurrection, for a moment there crossed my mind that after a lifetime of "becoming" a Christian, now at last I had finally become one. But the thought no sooner came than it went, because now there was no one left to BE a Christian. For a moment this was as bewildering as having a hard won ribbon snatched away. But suddenly there was Christ—who was never a Christian! As the divine underlying everyone's reality, Christ belongs to no one, not even to himself. In the end, then, there is just Christ, and no one to be a Christian.

BUDDHISM
The Diamond Sutra

THIS CHAPTER INCLUDES AN INTRODUCTION TO *The Diamond Sutra*, A selection of verses, and a brief analysis of the sutra by Wei Wu Wei.

INTRODUCTION BY A. F. PRICE

The original of the Jewel of Transcendental Wisdom is a Sanskrit text called the Vajrachchedika-prajnaparamita-sutra. The Vajrachchedika (Diamond Cutter) is a small book belonging to the Mahaprajnaparamita (Perfection of Transcendental Wisdom). It may be called a classic, a scripture, or a discourse, as all these three terms are comprehended in the Sanskrit word sutra, the appellation given to the sacred books of the Buddhist canon.

The Perfection of Transcendental Wisdom, one of the many books in the great canon of Mahayana (or Northern) Buddhism, is by far the largest, running into a great number of volumes. Many of the books of which this canon is made up are written in the form of dialogues between the Buddha and one or other of his chief disciples; but in point of fact these dialogues are not likely to be records of actual discourses. The Buddha left no written testament, and though records were made from memory by his followers some years after his passing, many parts of the Northern canon are of much later date. It is generally considered by the faithful that these later works enshrine the deep teachings of their lord, and that these teachings were passed down orally from generation to generation among those elect who proved the truths for themselves by practice. Precisely why, when, and by whom this oral transmission came to be set down in symbols cannot be stated with certainty, but research may provide these data at any moment.

The writings here concerned are generally considered to be the work of the profound and saintly fourteenth patriarch, Nagarjuna, who lived in the second century C.E.; but it would seem wiser to take the view that there was a succession of authors and compilers extending over a period of several hundred years from the first century B.C.E., and that the Diamond Cutter was written in the fourth century C.E. Although it forms so small a part of the Perfection of Transcendental Wisdom, its importance lies in its being an epitome of the whole. It is therefore extremely profound and extremely subtle.

The Diamond Sutra

A few of the 32 verses of *The Diamond Sutra* are included here. Selected notes are included as small text at the end of some verses.

I. The Convocation of the Assembly

Thus have I heard. Upon a time Buddha sojourned in Anathapindika's Park by Shravasti with a great company of *bhikshus*, even twelve hundred and fifty.

One day, at the time for breaking fast, the World-Honored One enrobed, and carrying his bowl, made his way into the great city of Shravasti to beg for his food. In the midst of the city he begged from door to door according to rule. This done, he returned to his retreat and took his meal. When he had finished he put away his robe and begging bowl, washed his feet, arranged his seat, and sat down.

bhikshu: a religious mendicant or friar of the order founded by Gotama Buddha

II. Subhuti Makes a Request

Now in the midst of the assembly was the Venerable Subhuti. Forthwith he arose, uncovered his right shoulder, knelt upon his right knee, and, respectfully raising his hands with palms joined, addressed Buddha thus: World-Honored One, it is most precious how mindful the Tathagata is of all the bodhisattvas, protecting and instructing them so well! World-Honored One, if good men and good women seek the consummation of incomparable enlightenment, by what criteria should they abide and how should they control their thoughts?

Buddha said: Very good, Subhuti! Just as you say, the Tathagata is ever mindful of all the bodhisattvas, protecting and instructing them well. Now listen and take my words to heart: I will declare to you by what criteria good men and good women seeking the consummation of incomparable enlightenment should abide, and how they should control their thoughts.

Said Subhuti: Pray, do, World-Honored One. With joyful anticipation we long to hear.

Tathagata: a title of the Buddha. The discourse itself later unfolds the meaning.
bodhisattva: an advancing devotee of enlightenment

III. The Real Teaching of the Great Way

Buddha said: Subhuti, all the bodhisattva heroes should discipline their thoughts as follows: All living creatures of whatever class, born from eggs, from wombs, from moisture, or by transformation, whether with form or without form, whether in a state of thinking or exempt from thought necessity, or wholly beyond all thought realms—all these are caused by me to attain unbounded liberation nirvana. Yet when vast, uncountable, immeasurable numbers of beings have thus been liberated, verily no being has been liberated. Why is this, Subhuti? It is because no bodhisattva who is a real bodhisattva cherishes the idea of an ego entity, a personality, a being, or a separated individuality.

IV. Even the Most Beneficent Practices Are Relative

Furthermore, Subhuti, in the practice of charity a bodhisattva should be detached. That is to say, he should practice charity without regard to appearances—without regard to sound, odor, touch, flavor or any quality. Subhuti, thus should the bodhisattva practice charity without attachment. Wherefore? In such a case his merit is incalculable.

Subhuti, what do you think? Can you measure all the space extending eastward?

No, World-Honored One, I cannot.

Then can you, Subhuti, measure all the space extending southward, westward, northward, or in any other direction, including nadir and zenith?

No, World-Honored One, I cannot.

Well, Subhuti, equally incalculable is the merit of the bodhisattva who practices charity without any attachment to appearances. Subhuti, bodhisattvas should persevere one-pointedly in this instruction.

V. Understanding the Ultimate Principle of Reality

Subhuti, what do you think? Is the Tathagata to be recognized by some material characteristic?

No, World-Honored One; the Tathagata cannot be recognized by any material characteristic. Wherefore? Because the Tathagata has said that material characteristics are not, in fact, material characteristics.

Buddha said: Subhuti, wheresoever are material characteristics there is delusion; but whoso perceives that all characteristics are in fact no-characteristics, perceives the Tathagata.

XIII. How this Teaching Should Be Received and Retained

At that time Subhuti addressed Buddha, saying: World-Honored One, by what name should this discourse be known, and how should we receive and retain it?

Buddha answered: Subhuti, this discourse should be known as The Diamond of the Perfection of Transcendental Wisdom—thus should you receive and retain it. Subhuti, what is the reason herein? According to the buddha-teaching the perfection of transcendental wisdom is not really such. "Perfection of transcendental wisdom" is just the name given to it. Subhuti, what do you think? Has the Tathagata a teaching to enunciate?

Subhuti replied to the Buddha: World-Honored One, the Tathagata has nothing to teach.

Subhuti, what do you think? Would there be many molecules in [the composition of] three thousand galaxies of worlds?

Subhuti said: Many indeed, World-Honored One!

Subhuti, the Tathagata declares that all these molecules are not really such; they are called "molecules." [Furthermore,] the Tathagata declares that a world is not really a world; it is [merely] called "a world."

Subhuti, what do you think? May the Tathagata be perceived by the thirty-two physical peculiarities [of an outstanding sage]?

No, World-Honored One, the Tathagata may not be perceived by these thirty-two marks. Wherefore? Because the Tathagata has explained that the thirty-two marks are not really such; they are [merely] called "the thirty-two marks."

Subhuti, if on the one hand a good man or a good woman sacrifices as many lives as the sand-grains of the Ganges, and on the other hand anyone receives and retains even only four lines of this discourse, and teaches and explains them to others, the merit of the latter will be the greater.

XIV. Perfect Peace Lies in Freedom from Characteristic Distinctions

Upon the occasion of hearing this discourse Subhuti had an interior realization of its meaning and was moved to tears. Whereupon he addressed the Buddha thus: It is a most precious thing, World-Honored One, that you should deliver this supremely profound discourse. Never have I heard such an exposition since of old my eye of wisdom first opened. World-Honored One, if anyone listens to this discourse in faith with a pure, lucid mind, he will thereupon conceive an idea of fundamental reality. We should know that such a one establishes the most remarkable virtue. World-Honored One, such an idea of fundamental reality is not, in fact, a distinctive idea; therefore the Tathagata teaches: "Idea of fundamental reality" is merely a name.

World-Honored One, having listened to this discourse, I receive and retain it with faith and understanding. This is not difficult for me, but in ages to come, in the last five-hundred years, if there be men coming to hear this discourse who receive and retain it with faith and understanding, they will be persons of most remarkable achievement. Wherefore? Because they will be free from the idea of an ego entity, free from the idea of a personality, free from the idea of a being, and free from the idea of a separated individuality. And why? Because the distinguishing of an ego entity is erroneous. Likewise the distinguishing of a personality, or a being, or a separated individuality is erroneous. Consequently those who have left behind every phenomenal distinction are called buddhas all.

Buddha said to Subhuti: Just as you say! If anyone listens to this discourse and is neither filled with alarm nor awe nor dread, be it known that such a one is of remarkable achievement. Wherefore? Because, Subhuti, the Tathagata teaches that the first perfection [the perfection of charity] is not, in fact, the first perfection: such is merely a name.

Subhuti, the Tathagata teaches likewise that the perfection of patience is not the perfection of patience: such is merely a name. Why so? It is shown thus, Subhuti: When the Rajah of Kalinga mutilated my body, I was at that time free from the idea of an ego entity, a personality, a being, and a separated individuality. Wherefore? Because then when my limbs were cut away piece by piece, had I been bound by the distinctions aforesaid, feelings of anger and hatred would have been aroused in me.

Subhuti, I remember that long ago, sometime during my past five hundred mortal lives, I was an ascetic practicing patience. Even then was I free from those distinctions of separated selfhood. Therefore, Subhuti, bodhisattvas should leave behind all phenomenal distinctions and awaken the thought of the consummation of incomparable enlightenment by not allowing the mind to depend upon notions evoked by the sensible world—by not allowing the mind to depend upon notions evoked by sounds, odors, flavors, touch contacts, or any qualities. The mind should be kept independent of any thoughts which arise within it. If the mind depends upon anything, it has no sure haven. This is why Buddha teaches that the mind of a bodhisattva should not accept the appearances of things as a basis when exercising charity. Subhuti, as bodhisattvas practice charity for the welfare of all living beings, they should do it in this manner. Just as the Tathagata declares that characteristics are not characteristics, so he declares that all living beings are not, in fact, living beings.

Subhuti, the Tathagata is he who declares that which is true; he who declares that which is fundamental, he who declares that which is ultimate. He does not declare that which is deceitful nor that which is monstrous. Subhuti, that Truth to which the Tathagata has attained is neither real nor unreal.

Subhuti, if a bodhisattva practices charity with mind attached to formal notions he is like a man groping sightless in the gloom; but a bodhisattva who practices charity with mind detached from any formal notions is like unto a man with open eyes in the radiant glory of the morning, to whom all kinds of objects are clearly visible.

Subhuti, if there be good men and good women in future ages, able to receive, read, and recite this discourse in its entirety, the Tathagata will clearly perceive and recognize them by means of his buddha-knowledge; and each one of them will bring immeasurable and incalculable merit to fruition.

The declarations of the Tathagata are concerned with principal truth, upon which all relative aspects—including the conformity of thought to things—depend. The idea of reality implies the idea of unreality, and vice versa. As each of these ideas suggests the other, they must be linked together in the mind, but by objective comparison they are contradictory. So worldly knowledge is dichotomizing, distinguishing, and estimating, but Tathagata-knowledge is formless, imageless, transcendental, and free from dualism.

XXXII. The Delusion of Appearances

Subhuti, someone might fill innumerable worlds with the seven treasures and give all away in gifts of alms, but if any good man or any good woman awakens the thought of Enlightenment and takes even only four lines from this discourse, reciting, using, receiving, retaining and spreading them abroad and explaining them for the benefit of others, it will be far more meritorious.

Now in what manner may he explain them to others? By detachment from appearances—abiding in real truth. So I tell you:

Thus shall ye think of all this fleeting world:

A star at dawn, a bubble in a stream;
A flash of lightning in a summer cloud,
A flickering lamp, a phantom, and a dream.

When the Buddha finished this discourse the venerable Subhuti, together with the *bhikshus, bhikshunis*, lay-brothers and sisters, and the whole realms of gods, men and titans, were filled with joy by his teaching, and, taking it sincerely to heart they went their ways.

Because It Is Not, by Wei Wu Wei

Wei Wu Wei, unless otherwise noted, quotes from the Edward Conze translation of *The Diamond Sutra.*

Authority is comforting; let us seek it. In Chapter 13 of the Diamond Sutra the Buddha takes a series of five examples—transcendental wisdom, his own teaching, particles of dust, the world-system, and the thirty-two marks of a superman. Of these it is said that they are, that they are not, and that therefore they are. For instance, "Because what was taught as particles of dust by the Tathagata, as not particles that was taught by the Tathagata. Therefore they are called 'particles of dust.' And this world-system the Tathagata has taught as no world-system. Therefore is it called a world-system." And so on for each.

This is followed by one of the elaborate hyperbolic metaphors used to emphasise the supreme importance of this teaching. And indeed the Venerable Subhuti is moved to tears thereby, and according to Mr. A. F. Price's translation from the Chinese, had "an interior realization" of its meaning. One might read this many times without understanding the tremendous importance attached to it, for neither translator draws attention to it or offers an explanation.

Nevertheless its supreme importance is evident enough when one understands that each of these contradictions is just an example of the formula "It is: because it is not, therefore it is," or, as I give it, "I (apparently) am: because I am not, therefore I am," or "Because Reality is Non-reality, therefore it is reality," "Since Being is Non-being, therefore it is Being."

The importance of this understanding of the precedence of the negative element to the positive, of the Void to the Plenum, of Non-being to Being, of I am not to I am, is sufficiently great to justify any degree of hyperbole—for it requires a reversal of our habitual way of regarding these matters, and a transvaluation of our established values according to which, as I have pointed out, we assume positive Reality or Being and then look for their negatives. That is, we imagine the Void as an emptiness in a pre-existing fullness, a nothing in an assumed Something, whereas we are urgently required to apprehend the ubiquitous pre-existence of Nothing out of which something may appear, or out of Non-manifestation manifestation.

In the following chapter, 14, Subhuti, full of enthusiasm, says, "Through it cognition has been produced in me. Not have I ever before heard such a discourse on *Dharma*. Most wonderfully blest will be those who, when this sutra is being taught, will produce a true perception. And that which is true perception, *that indeed is no perception*. Therefore the Tathagata teaches true perception." And again, in the same chapter, "This perception of a being, Subhuti, that is just a non-perception. Those all-beings of whom the Tathagata has spoken, they are indeed no-beings." And why? Because the Tathagata speaks *"in accordance with reality."* (Dr. Edward Conze, "The Diamond Sutra.")

"In accordance with reality" means in our vocabulary—since the term "reality" is so variously understood—"in accordance with the whole-mind."

It might not be too much to say that this, together with its counterpart the inexistence of any kind of self, is the *leitmotiv* of this sutra, capital in gnostic Buddhism, and constitutes perhaps its essential message. Subsequently indeed a considerably greater number of other "dharmas" are treated according to the same formula, one of the most direct of which is, "'Beings, beings', Subhuti, the Tathagata has taught that they are all no-beings. Therefore has he spoken of 'all beings.'" (Ch. 21)

It might be thought that what is meant is "I am and I am not, and only in that sense I am," but the words of the Buddha are very definite and are reiterated *ad nauseam* in the Hindu manner. He *taught* that things and concepts *(dharmas)* are not, and that is *why* things and concepts (dharmas) are.

But Vedanta Advaita teaches, "I am," and the Buddhist doctrine of the Void teaches "I am not." The Buddha makes it clear, again and again, that it is *on account of this latter teaching* that in a sense I can be.

It therefore seems apparent that there are three stages on this path. The pilgrim learns to *understand* that he is, after having understood that as an I-concept he is not. Then, and only then, he comes to *know* that nevertheless he is not, for nothing is, not even he. And finally he *realizes* that in consequence of that and in a sense inconceivable before, he is.

Hence the formula: I am: I am not, therefore I am.

The essential doctrine of the Diamond Sutra is that no sort or kind of self is to be considered as existing. Having disposed of the I-concept, the Buddha proceeds to dispose of the elements that serve as the basis for it, i.e., the five *skandhas*, and, finally, of all "dharmas" from the supreme doctrine of enlightenment, via all perceptions and the Four Holy Truths (the Heart Sutra here) down to his own physical body.

In short, as Hui Neng realized so early in life, nothing at all exists, which is the Void. But the Buddha always adds that therefore everything exists in some manner. The translations are unsatisfactory here, for some say "are said to exist" or "are called such and such," whereas others are less evasive. One might suspect that none quite gives the sense.

PART FOUR

Nondual Perspectives

WE HAVE APPROACHED DESIRE FROM THE NONDUAL PERSPECTIVE OF recognizing that we "are not." A dualistic perspective would assume "we are" and might include instructions on how to live a moral life, for example. We considered religions from the nondual perspective rather than from the dualistic viewpoint of heaven and hell, for example.

The nondual perspective isn't better or more advanced than the dualistic perspective. The nondual perspective, because it is a perspective, a view of something, is dualistic. By considering the oxymoron "nondual perspective," we get a keener sense of how things remain distinct while being non-separate. We investigate further in this part of the book.

In the next few chapters we'll read about psychotherapy, education, art, and the movie *The Matrix*, from the nondual perspective. Other writings from a variety of fields could have been included, such as ecofeminism, music, or physics. Entire volumes could be devoted to each of these perspectives. New genres could be developed, such as cinema nondualité. Nondual expressions of varying depth and quality can be found for probably all interests and fields of knowledge.

The authors in the current section could be called self-realized. They express their perception of nondual reality by discussing how it bears on activities in the world: becoming an artist, doing therapy, creating new kinds of schools for children, viewing a movie.

Buddhism offers teachings on how to live life in a way aligned with the teaching of nonduality. The Eightfold Path in Buddhism instructs us to hold all eight of these views at all times:

1. Right view—holding the nondual perspective and understanding the four noble truths, which assert that existence is suffering; craving is the cause of suffering; through the complete ending of craving, suffering can end; the way to end suffering is the eightfold path.

2. Right resolve—with right view, right action will follow; nonharmfulness to sentient beings, or acting not from the 'I'-thought or ego, but from alignment with Self.

3. Right speech—saying what needs to be said without causing harm or manipulating people.

4. Right action—acting with simplicity; avoiding complication and conflicts with moral discipline; taking responsibility to find the right answer to life problems and to do the work in front of us.

5. Right livelihood—doing work not harmful to or taking advantage of others. Our job or career does not have to be our life. It could be "just a job." We do our work simply and properly.

6. Right effort—no resistance, struggling, or aggression. Aligning with what is wholesome. Seeing things as they are and working with them in a gentle way.

7. Right mindfulness—attending with precision and clarity to all facets of our life: experiences, activities, jobs, people around us, our bodies, feelings, thoughts, the objects of thought. Everything without exception is recognized as arising from Self.

8. Right concentration—this is inquiry or surrender, as we have

learned from the teaching of Sri Ramana Maharshi. The stilling of the mind so that nondual reality or the Self is known. The focus of attention that leads to self-realization.

Right concentration takes us back to the main purpose of this book, which is how to follow through with our desire for nonduality.

If nonduality makes sense to us as a good perspective from which to live life, then it would be worthwhile to know who is living life that way, what they're doing, and why their work is significant.

John J. Prendergast provides an excellent introduction to nonduality and then shows how therapists may apply awakening nondual awareness in their practices. He says,

> [An] impact of an awakening nondual awareness is an enhanced capacity to be with *what is*. All mainstream schools of psychotherapy understand the importance of acceptance, yet the dualistic mind can never be an agent of complete acceptance. The mind only accepts *what is* conditionally, hoping that if something is accepted, it will change. The living insight of nondual awareness is that everything already is accepted and embraced just as it is. As awakening deepens, the judging mind loses its grip and attention becomes increasingly innocent, intimate, and impersonally affectionate.[1]

When it comes to educating our children, Steven Harrison calls for a focus upon awareness so that the information absorbed by children is integrated wholly:

> Awareness doesn't need more information. It needs only enough information. This intelligence, the quality that mediates information into wisdom, is seldom referenced in school. If we do not include awareness in what we convey to our children, then aren't we teaching them to be

> unconscious and to be consumers of an endless stream of pointless information and products?
>
> The young child inhabits a vast array of kinds of intelligence held in the body/mind. Their need for information is intense, but it is mediated by the other capacities of their system—their feelings, sensations, and body appetites for movement and play. We can channel all of their life energy into the absorption of information, but without the intelligence of the whole child, we will produce adults who have a great deal of fragmented data, but have integrated nothing.[2]

Later Harrison says, "The life of inquiry, the life of open learning, requires ... investigation of and contact with everything, just as it is."

Jerry Wennstrom is an artist living on Whidbey Island in Washington State. His story is one of surrender to God or Self:

> In 1979, I destroyed all the art I had created, gave everything I owned away, and began a new life. I sensed an inner and outer world in perfect order. I sensed that I could become a willing participant in that order, and that it allowed for my individual expression and unique contribution. I know now that my participation was conditional on how well I learned to listen and to see the inherent patterns within the natural order I sensed. The return of a physical creative expression came later, after I learned what was required by the inner life. The new life that I gave myself to required unconditional trust and noninterference. I asked for nothing from any human being. I needed to know if there was a God, and I risked my life to find that out. I know now that we risk far more when we attempt to create a life devoid of a personal relationship with our God.[3]

Pradheep Chhalliyil, a scientist living in Iowa, shows how the movie *The Matrix* depicts reality from the nondual perspective. The Matrix is a computer program that controls human minds. In the story, human beings are kept in pods, serving as energy sources for artificial intelligence. Their brains are connected to the Matrix program which allows people in pods to think they are living in a normal world in which they wake and sleep, date, marry, have jobs, etc. It is a life of unawareness of reality. Many live like that now in this world.

> Because every thought depends on the mind—the thinker—we become a slave to the mind. Every experience we go through, every impression we take-in molds our future thoughts and actions. As we go through life we program ourselves to accept a world that is not more real than the world of *The Matrix*. Our world becomes a Self-created reality with its own mind-created logic to justify it. Thus we lose our real freedom, our unbounded nature. If "happy" thoughts flow, we are happy. If "sad" thoughts flow, we are sad. All emotions are nothing but thoughts. If they get completely out of control we can even go insane. And it all seems so real![4]

As we read these accounts of nondual perspective, over and over again we will find accord with the practice of inquiry and surrender prescribed by Sri Ramana Maharshi. These perspectives are various ways of confessing or calling for a turn toward awareness, Self, God, our unbounded nature. That turning is the job of one who desires nonduality.

PSYCHOTHERAPY
The Sacred Mirror

John J. Prendergast

AT THE BEGINNING OF THE TWENTY-FIRST CENTURY WE ARE WITNESSING an increasingly intimate conversation between Western psychotherapists and teachers from the Eastern wisdom traditions.[1] This conversation has been happening simultaneously on a number of different levels. The most obvious and outward level is intellectual, evidenced by the growing stream of books and journal articles (mostly Buddhist), as well as by conferences and academic classes that include a Transpersonal or Integral orientation. However, a less obvious but more important part of this conversation is happening experientially and intuitively as psychotherapists sit silently in meditation and dialogue with Indian and Southeast Asian sages, Japanese and Korean Zen masters, Middle Eastern Sufis, Taoist masters,

Tibetan lamas and *rinpoches*, and more recently with some of their long-term Western students who have become teachers in their own right. In fact, this conversation between Eastern-oriented dharma teachers and Western psychotherapists is a smaller part of a much larger dialogue that includes millions of nonpsychotherapists as well as teachers in the Christian, Jewish, and native mystical traditions. In addition, increasing numbers of individuals in the West are reporting spontaneous and profound, life transforming awakenings without prior exposure to any spiritual teachers, teachings, or practices.[2] Surveying these developments, we see the emergence of an essential dialogue, stripped of its cultural forms and roles, between the conditioned mind and that awareness which is unconditioned, open, and unknown. Reality seems to be enjoying this conversation with itself, since it is happening with increasing frequency and depth.

The fruit of this dialogue has been an accelerated awakening of nondual wisdom. Nonduality is a rather curious and uncommon word that so far has been used by a relatively small number of scholars and teachers.[3] It derives from the Sanskrit word *advaita,* which means "not-two." Nondual wisdom refers to the understanding and direct experience of a fundamental consciousness that underlies the apparent distinction between perceiver and perceived. From the nondual perspective, the split between self and other is a purely mental construct. This understanding, rooted in the direct experience of countless sages through millennia, is at the heart of Hindu Vedanta, most schools of Buddhism, and Taoism, and mystical Christianity, Judaism, and Islam. Nonduality is a particularly elegant and clear formulation, since it describes reality in terms of what it is not (unsplit, undivided) rather than what it is. It has the added advantage of being nonsectarian, unhinged to any particular religious or psychospiritual tradition, yet adaptable to many. It is a word that points to that which is before and beyond the projections of a separative, self-reflexive mind. What is pointed to can never be adequately conceptualized. It can only be lived in the timeless now.

Nondual wisdom expresses itself as and through a radiant heart (love) and illumined mind (wisdom). While essentially without qualities, it is commonly experienced as being vast, free, spacious, heartfelt, and present-centered. Many people report feeling a subtle joy, love, compassion, peace, gratitude, and sense of connectedness with all of life when they directly attune with it. There are many signs that this awareness is emerging in the West. Why now? Perhaps it is as the historian Charles Beard (Rogers, 1980) observed, "When the skies grow dark, the stars begin to shine."

This flowering of nondual wisdom is presenting new challenges and opportunities for the field of psychotherapy. While Ken Wilber (2000, 1996) and other Integral/Transpersonal philosophers and psychologists have mapped out nondual awareness as the pinnacle of self-realization, it has been presented as a rarefied condition. Surprisingly, this no longer appears to be as true. As a result, a new generation of clinicians and teachers has begun to explore how this awareness directly impacts the way psychotherapists work.

The Sacred Mirror refers to the capacity of the therapist to reflect back the essential nature of the client—that awareness that is prior to and inclusive of all thoughts, feelings, and sensations. Sacred mirroring is multidimensional, reflecting both personal and impersonal dimensions of being. This capacity implies a high degree of maturity by therapists who are awakening to the realization that they are not only who they have taken themselves to be. They realize, at least to some degree, that they are not limited to being a "therapist" (although they may function in that role), or even a "person." Their locus of identity is either resting in or moving toward unconditioned awareness, or Presence. The result is the emergence of a natural simplicity, transparency, clarity, and warm acceptance of whatever arises within themselves and their clients. Since they increasingly do not take themselves as some "thing," they also do not take their clients as objects separate from themselves. They understand that there is no separate mirror and someone mirrored; there is only mirroring. As Rumi (1995) said, "We are the mirror, as well as the face in it."

Through their Presence and skillful therapeutic means, awakening psychotherapists may spontaneously assist some of their clients to see through their various limited identities and gradually rest in an unknown openness, even as they fully honor, accept, and explore whatever mental, emotional, and somatic contractions arise. This expansive role complements and increasingly overlaps with the traditional role of the spiritual teacher or director, and raises a number of interesting questions.

First, we may ask whether we are witnessing the emergence of a new school of psychotherapy—one that is "nondual." Certainly one could reasonably propose this. Perhaps a modern set of principles and practices that enhance awakening and transformation could be articulated and taught. Maybe, as spiritual teacher Peter Fenner suggests, nondual therapy is what the sages, Buddha included, have been doing all along and we are simply encountering an old wine—Buddhadharma—in a new wineskin. On the other hand, there are good reasons to be cautious about trying to codify or reify nondual awareness into yet another framework that will eventually be added to the compost pile along with all of the psychological models that preceded it. By its nature, that which is nondual is undivided and nonconceptual. The conceptual mind can never nail it down. It is not limited by a set of principles since it is the source of all principles. Nor can it be confined to any particular set of practices, since reality uses all tools at its disposal at any given moment, including death, disease, pain, shock, and suffering, to point us to our true nature. Nonduality can never be confined by any philosophy or psychospiritual practice, although such practices may play a vital role in preparing the ground for awakening or facilitating a glimpse of our true nature. It is not limited to any object or subtle state of consciousness, even as it includes these. It is both no-thing and everything, empty yet full of pure potentiality. It is immanent and transcendent, formed and formless. And it is none of this. It is *what is* and *what we are* and little more of any meaning can be said about it. Mainly we can describe what it is not, and even that in time will be seen to be untrue.

Even though nondual awareness cannot be objectified, awakening to it changes one's life profoundly. How may we assess its impact on the field of psychotherapy? It may be helpful to think of psychotherapy, and all of life for that matter, as having a horizontal and vertical dimension. The horizontal refers to the realm of form—the evolution of phenomenal life in time and space. The vertical refers to that which is formless and exists outside of time and space. Psychology, like all disciplines, evolves on the horizontal plane as new information about the development and functioning of the human body/mind is discovered and synthesized, leading to new schools of thought. While the *concept* of nondual awareness has already been incorporated horizontally into transpersonal and Integral frameworks, its main effect occurs vertically as practitioners deepen in their intimacy with their true nature.

Awakening nondual awareness adds a depth dimension to any of the existing schools of psychology, regardless of their orientation, through the psychotherapist's deepening awareness. Whether their model is neoanalytic (object relations, self psychology, intersubjectivity), Jungian, cognitive/behavioral, humanistic/existential, or Integral/Transpersonal, awakening psychotherapists bring a quality of awareness that transforms their work. It is not so much that therapists integrate Being, as they are absorbed by it. As they more deeply attune with and embody the ground of Being, Presence is enhanced. Their thoughts, feelings, and actions tend to spontaneously radiate out from this open awareness. Authentic transformation arises from the therapist and client's coexploration of *what is.*

Presence can be described as Being aware of Itself. Its effects are contagious. When we are in the Presence of an individual who has awakened from the dream of "me," we can sense an unpretentiousness, lucidity, transparency, joy, and ease of being. Those same qualities are elicited within ourselves. What is normally background may temporarily be called into the foreground of attention. When Presence is particularly strong and we are particularly open, it may feel as if a fire has been ignited. The German-Canadian sage Eckhart Tolle (1999) has commented on this:

> When a log that has only just started to burn is placed next to one that is burning fiercely, and after a while they are separated again, the first log will be burning with much greater intensity. After all, it is the same fire. To be such a fire is one of the functions of a spiritual teacher. Some

> therapists may also be able to fulfill that function, provided they have gone beyond the level of mind and can create and sustain a state of intense conscious presence while they are working with you.

Tolle's proviso that therapists must transcend the mind is critically important.

Does this mean that psychotherapy is evolving into a Western vehicle for the transmission of the flame of dharma, or truth? Are awakening psychotherapists in the same lineage as the Buddha or India's other illustrious sages? It seems obvious that any awakening or awakened beings will transmit their understanding according to their capacities and limitations in any moment. This holds true for psychotherapists and nonpsychotherapists alike. In some ways being a psychotherapist may make awakening more difficult, especially if there are strong attachments to theories about the mind. On the other hand, psychotherapists are in a unique position in modern society to offer a sanctuary for individuals to sort out their lives and more intimately explore their direct experience. Further, people may be more at ease working individually with a therapist who has a nondual orientation than with joining a spiritual organization or community that has its own specialized rules, roles, and rituals.

Having identified the flowering of Presence as the primary impact of awakening, we can also recognize a number of powerful secondary effects. One obvious area is in our self-identity as a "psychotherapist." When we awaken from the sense of personal identity, we also awaken from all of our role identities, even as these roles continue. We are like the actor who snaps out of his trance while onstage and suddenly realizes that he had lost himself in his role. Even though we continue our roles as Mr. or Ms. Jones, we do not forget that it is just a play. Therapy is what we do, it is not who we are. As a result, we take ourselves much more lightly. The role of psychotherapist has its legitimate and socially relevant function, yet we no longer allow it to become a screen or mask to hide behind. Freed of the role identity, we are more authentic, transparent, available, and creative in the moment. We are no longer problem solvers facing problem holders. Instead, we are Being meeting itself in one of its infinite and intriguing disguises.

If we no longer take ourselves as problem solvers, it is also true that we can no longer find any real problems. This radical understanding can be disorienting. Clearly, nearly all clients come in presenting problems that therapists are taught to carefully assess in their initial sessions. If there is no problem, what is there to do? We meet the client where they are. If they believe that they have a problem, and certainly there will be compelling evidence to support such an interpretation, we join them there and begin the process of intimately exploring what the actual experience of the "problem" is. As apparent problems are gradually unpacked and clients deepen in their self-intimacy, they will eventually encounter a profound sense of emptiness that has been fiercely defended against. They discover that their prior problems were all outcomes from and compensatory expressions of this defense against what at first appears to be annihilation and in time reveals itself as unconditional love. When we believe that we are not enough, we think, feel, and act in all kinds of ways that create suffering for ourselves and others. Yet even this avoidance of emptiness is not seen as a problem. It is simply a misunderstanding of our true nature that is fundamentally empty—of everything we have taken to be true about ourselves and the world. This misunderstanding is also part of the divine play. Facing emptiness either will or will not occur depending upon the motivation and readiness of the client. It is not up to the therapist, who is free of any agenda, to change things as they are.

Another impact of an awakening nondual awareness is an enhanced capacity to be with what is. All mainstream schools of psychotherapy understand the importance of acceptance, yet the dualistic mind can never be an agent of complete acceptance. The mind only accepts what is conditionally, hoping that if something is accepted, it will change. The living insight of nondual awareness is that everything already is accepted and embraced just as it is. As awakening deepens, the judging mind loses its grip and attention becomes increasingly innocent, intimate, and impersonally affectionate. Attention drops from the head to the heart. Without any conscious intention on the part of the therapist, an optimal field of loving acceptance arises that facilitates transformation. What has been unmet is waiting to be fully embraced before it can transform. Unconditional love is the greatest transformative power. A flower bud naturally unfolds to the caress of sunlight; it cannot be willed to open.

Awakening nondual awareness fully discloses the therapeutic encounter as a shared field and enhances the phenomenon of empathic resonance (Hart, 2000). When we are no longer protecting and projecting a personal identity, we are multidimensionally open and available to our clients. A remarkable intimacy may evolve, depending in part upon the availability of the client, where we are able to experience our client's world as if from the inside. Interpersonal boundaries become very fluid and permeable yet without the merging and confusion that is typical of unconscious relationships. The therapist intimately experiences without becoming identified with or caught in whatever is being experienced, a blending of love and wisdom. We can touch the core of a client's contraction even as we retain a sense of spacious detachment. Interestingly, clients consciously participate in these encounters, knowing when a therapist's heart and sensitivity have touched them where they have never been met before. This empathic resonance helps heal the pain of separation.

The awakening of nondual awareness also facilitates the depth and transformative power of inquiry (the investigation into one's fundamental nature). Discernment is significantly enhanced. As therapists learn to live in the unknown, increasingly free of conclusions, they are better able to assist their clients to do the same. They see thoughts for what they are—just thoughts, recognizing the different layers of their clients' stories and assisting in their gradual deconstruction when this is appropriate. They know the peace and freedom of living without attachment to any story of how things are or should be. This is especially the case with the story of being a separate self, which is unquestioned by all conventional psychotherapies. The unfolding of nondual awareness allows therapists to authentically pose or support the investigation of essential questions such as

"Who am I?" "What do I really want?" and "Is it true?" and follow the process of undoing fundamental beliefs to their end beyond the conceptual mind. This is in marked contrast to the process of purely cognitive or intellectual inquiry that stays limited to the surface, rational mind. The illumined intellect (buddhi in Sanskrit) shines more freely as nondual awareness awakens to itself, allowing a natural resting in non-knowing.

We should also briefly address the issue of methods and skills. Since nondual awareness is all-inclusive, it will at times use skillful means to assist its own unfolding. Wisdom and love work through many "little methods." In psychotherapy this may look like silent listening, empathic reflections, inquiries, interpretations, educating through teaching stories and metaphors, invitations to be attentive to something, or to look, listen, or sense in a new way. Therapy can use nature, breath work, movement, bilateral stimulation, dream work, free association, toning, gazing, journaling, art, or a gentle touch of the hand. When effective, it almost always engages the body on some level. The critical question is whether the therapist's awareness is centered in the moment and creatively responsive to what is. Are we entering a session fixed to an agenda and protocol, or are we able to let everything go and be fresh and truly available? Can we let the session be naked and unfurnished at any moment? Are we able to rest in the Unknown?

The Sacred Mirror is primarily about how awakening impacts the psychotherapist and secondarily about how it affects psychotherapy. Yet awakening is not something that the conditioned mind can "do." It is out of the ego's control and happens of its own. We cannot pretend to be awake when we are not (this is still part of being in the dream of a separate self), nor can we completely deny or refuse our underlying nature as Awakeness. When awakening happens, it is an impersonal event and belongs to no one. It is *from*, not *for* the person. As the European sage Jean Klein (1988) observes, "Awakening happens when we are convinced that there is no one who awakens." It is enough to be where we are, as we are—lucidly allowing our experience in the moment, whether we are at war or peace with reality. The love of truth, manifesting as the surrender to Silence and an active investigation into all of our cherished beliefs, gradually leads us to greater authenticity. The rest takes care of itself. Living this way brings a sense of transparency to our lives and our work as psychotherapists. In time and without any conscious effort or intent we become like stained glass, more adequate forms of transmission of light. Our individuality is liberated and enhanced as we knowingly share this common ground with all beings.[4]

EDUCATION
Changing the Heart of Education

Steven Harrison

In times of change, learners inherit the earth, while the learned find themselves beautifully equipped to deal with a world that no longer exists.

—Eric Hoffer

IN ALL THE DISCUSSION ABOUT HOW BEST TO TEACH CHILDREN, WE don't often hear about the purpose of education other than as a social obligation and the preparation of the child for the adult world of work. We don't hear much about the child, and almost nothing *from* the child.

Perhaps all that education aspires to be is the preparation of the young person for their role in the larger society. This is certainly a good idea for society, but in the efficiency of producing citizen workers, are we missing the deeper meaning and higher purpose of learning? Have we forgotten about the spirit of the child, the unique and fragile expression of a passionate and integrated life?

[*The Happy Child*] is about a reorientation of education, a radical and fundamental realignment of the purpose of education. Can education shift from its current model of shaping children into components of economic production, into an active experiment in optimizing the creativity of the whole child? We have been so busy educating our children that we have missed the heart of education, the creation of a happy life. A happy life, after all, is not only what we would like for our children, but for ourselves as well.

A happy person, fulfilled in their connection to their friends, family, and community and in the expression of their vocation, is likely to be useful and productive in their life and to help weave the collective fabric of a functional society. What else should a society need from education other than the happiness of its people? What else should we demand for our children other than their happiness?

NOTHING: WHAT YOU'VE BEEN LOOKING FOR

Sometimes you can observe a lot by watching.

—Yogi Berra

When we teach children that information is the most important element in an education, we are subtly selling them on a value system that is imbedded in our culture. Information has decreasing utility. Over time, much of what we learn becomes dated or irrelevant. Our world has too much information and not enough context. What serves our children is not simply endless streams of information, but the intelligence to organize and utilize it. It is the relationship to information, not information itself, that defines intelligence.

The information overload in our schools is a reflection of a culture that is obsessed with information and commerce, or information as commerce. Stock market quotes run across our television screens as we watch the news; in-between are commercials for products we are just learning we need. We scan the newspaper before we drive to work, listening to the news while we drive.

What is it we are looking for? We are accumulating information at an ever-increasing rate, but what is the point of it all? In the ongoing frenzy of discovering and recording more and more information, we have lost the context, the motivation behind the action.

This is the brave new world of information saturation, where data is bought and sold, where the individual is reduced to a statistical buying pattern. The message is consumption, and the medium is everything from the names of our sports stadiums to the pockets of the shirts we wear. There is nothing that isn't a commodity if it is packaged and sold. There is even a market for nothing, if you know how to sell it.

A short time ago in New Zealand, a young graphic designer was thinking about advertising and all its strangeness, its coercive ability to sell the most completely bizarre things to people who usually don't need them. He created a brilliant social experiment.

The designer considered what the most nonexistent product would be and decided to market … Nothing™. With billboards all over Auckland touting, "Nothing™—What you've been waiting for," and carrying the obligatory image of a beautiful woman looking off into the distance, the phones began to ring with callers who were ready to buy what they already presumably had plenty of.

The Nothing™ campaign showed something about the power of money to sell, the power of image to communicate a need that consumers did not even realize they had. Perhaps, most importantly, it demonstrated that even nothing could become something in the world of information.

If nothing can become something, then how do we know that everything isn't nothing? What if everything is simply packaged nothing that has been cleverly inserted into our minds as not just important, but essential? What if everything is nothing bundled up with attractive images and sold to us as ... what we've been looking for?

That is the promise of information. It tells us that what we are looking for is more, better, total information. This is the core of our contemporary education. If we can pack in enough information, we will have everything.

What if everything is not really what we've been looking for? What if the marketing of information has convinced us to accumulate more of everything, more of nothing, more of anything? What if none of that is what we are looking for? Yet we educate our children as if the endless stream of information is what they should be looking for.

The culture of endless marketing churns on, relentlessly.

Every place we look we see the corporate logo. More™. More™ Stadium. Brought to you by More™ (so you will buy more). Designed by More™. Sponsored by More™. And there's more.

Billboards that show a beautiful woman or a muscled young man with the slogan, "More™ ... What you've been looking for." Or simply: "Buy More™."

And when we look at these messages, what do we experience? Do we feel that somehow we are missing something if we don't have more? Or do we have the unsettling feeling that the message, the medium, the information-as-its-delivery is unrelated to what we are in fact looking for?

Do we actually feel that if small is beautiful, then less is joyous? Do we look at the information streaming towards us from all directions, and like futurist Aikido masters, let the information flow on by into the nether world of Nothing™?

What happens to the message when the medium is awareness? What if our counter-marketing campaign is "Awareness™ ... What we're looking from?"

Awareness doesn't need more information. It needs only enough information. This intelligence, the quality that mediates information into wisdom, is seldom referenced in school. If we do not include awareness in what we convey to our children, then aren't we teaching them to be unconscious and to be consumers of an endless stream of pointless information and products?

The young child inhabits a vast array of kinds of intelligence held in the body/mind. Their need for information is intense, but it is mediated by the other capacities of their system—their feelings, sensations, and body appetites for movement and play. We can channel all of their life energy into the absorption of information, but without the intelligence of the whole child, we will produce adults who have a great deal of fragmented data, but have integrated nothing.

Don't Trust Anyone over Three

A preschooler's tacit knowledge of grammar is more sophisticated than the thickest style manual or the most state-of-the-art computer language system.

—Steven Pinker

Anyone who has been around young children knows that this is the age of relentless inquiry. The world is fresh at three, if somewhat sociopathic. The big questions are simple at this age and they all boil down to one simple query: "Why?"

As adults around these little question machines, we often see our job as supplying answers to these questions. This role of holder-of-all-the-answers is soon made absurd by questions for which we can find no answers, exasperation with seemingly endless curiosity, and the pressure we start to feel to actually get something done.

"Take your socks off, please."

"Why?"

"Because they are wet."

"Why?"

"Because you stepped in a puddle."

"Why?"

"Because you wanted to."

"Why?"

"Take off your socks, now."

And, of course, it goes on all day, every day like this.

We often mistake this behavior of the three-year-old for that of someone looking for answers. We have usually forgotten what this state of profound curiosity is really about. As adults, we inhabit a concrete world of relative certainty, and we assume that this is what the child is looking for.

This is why you shouldn't trust anyone over three.

Young children are simply curious. Learning something doesn't fulfill their interest. This thirst cannot be quenched by answers. They want to know more, regardless of what they have found out so far. Their question in life is their life.

We can't answer their question.

We can, however, join them in their question. That would require us to abandon all our answers. We might lose track of time. We might not get anything done today. There may be no point to the question at all. The whole thing may be totally pointless, like a game without a score, without a conclusion, without a ... winner.

Maybe it's time to get some structured play going, with rules and some competition; after all, that is what these kids are going to face in life. Why do they want to spend so much time just playing?

Or, we could teach them that there is an answer to most questions and when there is no answer, then it is time to do something else besides ask these incessant questions. Over time, we can teach them to wonder less, to give up their questioning more easily, and to accept answers as conclusions, and then they will be well prepared to go to school. After school, they can live a productive life. And we can get back to what we were doing, which is no doubt pretty important.

And what if this questioning was cultivated, not quenched? What is the potential of a child whose curiosity knows no bounds? What would become of us as parents? What would become of our answers? What would become of our world?

We seem apprehensive of our children and their relentless drive to discover, their unfettered energy and clear eyes. Have we lost this quality so completely in our lives that we have forgotten its value?

Will the world we have constructed withstand their gaze?

If we do not give our lives over to this drive for discovery in our children and in ourselves, if we restrict our children to the answers we have already formulated, it leaves us with one simple question.

Why?

To address this question in our own being we can undergo an experiment. It is helpful to get a good night's sleep before proceeding with this. Contact a friend who has a young child or, better, several young children. (If you have your own children you can skip this experiment—you've already got your own going on. Just go for the good night's sleep.) Spend a full day with the child or children, not as an adult caretaker, but as a playmate. Play without conditions. Play when you take a snack break and a lunch.

Just play.

Everything in your environment is part of the game. There is no world outside of the immediate environment. There are no complicated relationships. There are no bills to pay. There is just play.

Do you find this free-form fun exhilarating, exhausting, or both? Do you tend to form rules? Do you look for meaning in the play? Do you want to accomplish something? When your play day is over, what is your state of mind? What does your adult world look like? What does the child's world look like? Try this for an hour or for a day. If you are really serious, then try it for the rest of your life. Ask yourself "Why?" Don't answer the question. Don't stop asking the question.

The Profound Knowledge of Not Knowing

The chief cause of problems is solutions.

—Milton Berle

When Socrates was faced with the challenge of who amongst his peers had come to the most profound knowledge, he blew away the competition with this irony: Socrates said that his was the greatest knowledge, because his knowledge was that he did not know.

We now study Socrates as one of history's spectacular minds, while most of his philosophical contemporaries have receded into a dim history, their once grand insights now just the subject of obscure philosophy courses.

Socrates' perception was a profound understanding of the nature of learning that led him to communicate through dialogue and to discourse using the medium of questions. As one of the greatest teachers of all time, Socrates suggested that there was nothing to teach and nothing to learn, and that the knowledge of life was inherently present in each person. The question simply revealed what was already known.

In Socrates' time, teachers—known as Sophists—gathered students by means of impressive promises of knowledge and elaborate philosophies—for a fee. Teachers were paid only if the students stayed, so the Sophists generally gave long-winded, self-assured discourses using reason to prove just about anything. Their legacy is the term *sophistry*, meaning deceptive reasoning, and their shadow still falls on education today.

Socrates, in yet another expression of his greatness, refused all fees for his teaching and continued to challenge the veracity and integrity of sophistry. He was eventually put to death for his outspokenness, sending a clear signal to everyone else that those in power would rather not deal with too many questions.

Thousands of years later, Socrates' questions and death still resonate through our cultural milieu. Today, our educational institutions have largely forgotten the importance of the question and have supported new and complex forms of sophistry. Those in power have continued to make clear that questions are not in favor.

And while few would suggest that public education is not failing, fewer still would point to the suppression of the question as the causative factor. The debate continues between vouchers and general funding, between teaching fundamental curricula and teaching broad-based curricula, between outcome-based education and esteem-based education. But all this debate is within the realm of sophistry, amongst those who promise knowledge as a result of their elaborate philosophies, and whose power—and income—is based on their position in the debate.

What if they are all wrong? What if the problem with education is that it is in the way of the question? What if there is no such thing as "too many questions?" What if Socrates was right?

If Socrates was right, then the question is the teacher, school, and textbook. The whole structure of educational institutions is missing the point. There is no need for answers when there are real questions. In a question-based education there can be no curriculum, no course work, and no tests, because a question is open-ended, unformatted, and without boundaries.

A question is alive; an answer is not. Perhaps this is why schools are failing. They are full of answers. Questions fitting those answers are encouraged, tested, and rewarded. Questions not fitting those answers are disciplined, drugged, or expelled.

Public education was designed to put skilled labor into the workplace. Asking questions does not keep the assembly line moving, so education taught skills, not creativity. Industry once required such labor, but now it is less clear that this kind of worker is needed. Computers and automation continue to eliminate repetitive jobs that require only noncritical thinking. What industry is beginning to notice is that it lacks creative labor: decision makers, designers, innovators. And it is no wonder that this is the case, since public education is still functioning on principles based on its founding in the Industrial Revolution. We are in the Information Age, hurtling towards what is next. Ages are being compressed in time. Where the Industrial Age was a few hundred years, the Information Age may be measured in decades. Machines now are the heart of industry and are clearly better at storing and sorting information. There is a small window of time in which creative intelligence is still an area of human dominance, but it is just a matter of time before machines acquire complex understanding and responses superior to our own. Machines are faster; synapses are simply slower.

Then what is the purpose of education in the face of this imminent obsolescence of human intelligence? We continue to teach information when that game is already over. That is because education has nothing else it knows how to do. Education itself is obsolete but is ignorant of that fact. It needs to be educated.

Meanwhile, the creativity, the exploration, the inquiry of our young are, like Socrates, being metaphorically executed by the powerful structures of our societal paradigm for asking too many questions.

Socrates might suggest a question: "Does anything need to be done to educate the question already residing in a child?"

Spirituality and Learning

We have all been schooled to have no inner life at all.

—John Gatto

We have accepted the indoctrination of cultural constructs as education and, more than that, we fear that if our children miss this enculturation they will have a miserable life. Whether it is the "Great Books" of the now out-of-fashion Liberal Arts education or the math/science obsession of the brave new techno world, a specific curriculum is a modeling of what the educated person should be and, more importantly, how that person will function in society.

The parent fears for their child and so gives the child over to these forces of homogeny and social cohesion. The price is the loss of the creative and passionate expression of the child (which is unlearned through the child's education). What is purchased is security. We fear that if we do not enroll our children in this behavior modification programming, then they will face hardship and failure. They will stick out. They will not have the skills or discipline to fit in, be productive, be employed, and so forth. Failed children mean we have failed. This is what our parents feared. And their parents.

By living our own lives (of which our children are an integral part) with tremendous passion, we face our fear rather than pass it on to the next generation, and we begin to put into place social forms that reflect a life of love and inquiry: intentional living communities; student-directed schools; cooperative, entrepreneurial, sustainable businesses; ecologically sound food production; relationship-based charity; artistic and media expressions that reflect more than materialism. Such a life is full of books and computers, paintbrushes and musical instruments, mystics and visionaries, along with entrepreneurs, artisans, scientists, and scholars. How could a child not be educated in a family, in a community, where life is fully lived?

While home schooling may address my child's needs, it does not address the larger question of meeting every child's needs. Home schooling may be necessary for the well being of my child because there is no alternative, but the possibility always exists of creating that alternative, for my child and for every child.

Pragmatically, the world is as it is, not as we might describe it in its ideal. We face a different kind of challenge in making sure that our life, which may be full of educational riches, is a shared life. The learning community extends our personal resources into the community at large so that any child who cares to can access the education they choose. The focus of a learning community is on a school center because our communities are not mature enough to provide a more natural, free-flowing, and integrated unschooling. Perhaps this was the ideal of public education, but not public education as it is.

The practical expression of the spiritual realization that life is interconnected is expressed in the forms we create, the work in progress of that understanding. Even a learning center that embodies freedom and responsibility is not complete until it seamlessly interfaces with the community of families, businesses, and institutions that surround it, as well as the world at large. Learning may finally be deinstitutionalized and returned to its natural state: curiosity-driven, lifelong, and incorporating every dimension of the human being.

All of this is theoretical unless we are actively living it, demonstrating it, and infusing all of what we say into all of what we live. The experiment of life may require a certain kind of refined space, but it must also be porous and interactive with the world at large. Without that openness, the experiment becomes stale and self-involved. Without doubt, we can create a bubble world for ourselves and those close to us, especially the children, but that is neither community nor educational, in the holistic sense. A closed alternative world is just the shadow side of the mainstream culture, and is part and parcel of it. The life of inquiry, the life of open learning, requires that investigation of and contact with everything, just as it is.

We all have the capacity to be still in the midst of the ten thousand forms, simply because all forms are, in fact, connected—not through those myriad forms, but through our common consciousness. Rather than try to sort the forms for the ones that please and avoid the ones that do not, is it possible for our simple awareness to move through the forms of our life, bringing with it whatever change or integration is necessary? Who is willing to step from the virtual world of safe spirituality into the life of passionate inquiry and pragmatic application of an experimental life? This is the challenge, not only for our children, but also for each of us, and all of life.

ART
An Artist's Journey of Transformation

Jerry Wennstrom

I BECAME NOTHING

In 1979, I destroyed all the art I had created, gave everything I owned away, and began a new life. I sensed an inner and outer world in perfect order. I sensed that I could become a willing participant in that order, and that it allowed for my individual expression and unique contribution. I know now that my participation was conditional on how well I learned to listen and to see the inherent patterns within the natural order I sensed. The return of a physical creative expression came later, after I learned what was required by the inner life. The new life that I gave myself to required unconditional trust and noninterference. I asked for nothing from any human being. I needed to know if there was a God, and I risked my life to find that out. I know now that we risk far more when we attempt to create a life devoid of a personal relationship with our God.

I ate when I had food and I fasted when I did not. I accepted whatever came into my life. It was that simple. I was familiar with fasting; I had done it once a week since I was twenty years old. Now, eating became a miracle. At first, I had something of a small following as an artist, and people were still interested in what I did, so they gave to me. Soon it became apparent that I was not going back into art, and many of these people faded from my life. I had a close circle of friends of the spirit who understood what I had given myself to, to some extent. They had their doubts, and so did I. My life was just too much for our modern western mind to consider. Eventually I saw the ways in which the miracle carried my life. I could never have continued this strange and lonely journey if I had not seen that. My joy and my ability to help others were gifts of that miracle and were my only tools for disarming the fears that were inevitably projected onto me. Fielding the fears of others was probably the most difficult task of the new life. I had to confront the fears within myself first. I had to give to others unconditionally and expect nothing in return. This is a society where everything is not enough.

On the surface, I looked like what most of us put all of our energies into avoiding. *I became nothing*. I had chosen to make an intuitive and conscious leap into the void so I did not have the luxury of asking for sympathy when the journey became frightening or impossible. Even the least intelligent among us would have suggested that I get a job and feed myself. I knew that I did not have that choice. I knew that once I jumped into the vast and empty ocean I saw before me, there was no measure in between that could save me. I would swim or drown. In water up to my neck, no choices and no turning back would be possible. I knew this was real.

In the cyclical rhythm of life, we eventually come up against a profound moment in which we must decide how much faith and courage we are willing to give ourselves to. Most often, in deciding this, we also establish how much courage we will live with for the rest of our lives. This crucial point usually comes to us at around the age of thirty. The opportunities at that time are like no other. Only the rare human being can leap into a deeper faith beyond that opportune stage in their life. Usually, if we have not done it under the best of circumstances, when the physical and spiritual winds are at our back, then we rarely find courage or reason enough to do it later in life. However, grace has no limits, and this is not written in stone. Only we know what we do with that moment once it arrives in our life, or where we may have set it to rest. Have we chosen the safe life, its foundation rooted in fear? Or have we chosen the Mystery, in which all may be lost or gained? We have only our inner knowing, and as an external indicator, the miracle, which informs us of the power of our choice. No one can judge, yet everyone intuits our choice by the ways in which it resembles their own.

The Stalemate with Formlessness

However detached I may have become from the label "artist," I never lost sight of art's essential heartland, and I held a creative vision throughout my journey. My detachment from any particular religious affiliation did not preclude the essential spirituality of the journey. I hold true that the path lived attentively is a sacred path, and that the fundamental spirit of art is alive, well, and deeply esoteric. As does any spiritual path, art has the potential to deliver us into our own true *becoming*, which is identical to our world's becoming. Art expresses and defines the deep and collective spirit of our time.

The path I followed had an unseen form. It could never have carried with it the progressive levels of understanding or the timely, saving moments of grace with their essential material gifts if it did not have its own vast, intelligent form. This fluid form was often terrifying to my small human mind, as it grappled with the all-inclusive expansiveness of infinite possibility. When our small lives open outward to include *everything*, how do we make sense of it? What becomes important or unimportant, and how do we determine those differences? I knew that an order held life in balance, an unseen glue that I could not possess. I did not understand it, nor could I find comfort in this order, because of its inherently illusive nature. I could only trust the glue to hold—trust it with my life—which is what I did.

The way life was unfolding did not fit any religious form that I, or anyone else, knew how to define. This trust was all there was. People who have heard a little of my story ask me, "Were you a monk?" or "What particular tradition did you follow?" Over and over I come up against the same moment of emptiness that I have encountered from the beginning. What am I to say in answer to these sincere questions? "I listened for the moments when *that*, which contains the vastness of *everything*, specifically led me, one small and searching individual, somewhere in particular!" I seem to answer that question differently every time it is asked. I listen deeply for what the questioner needs to support his own journey and I answer accordingly.

Most of us seek a new relationship to the vastness of everything, a glimpse of formless freedom, as we move along our spiritual paths. We intuit a mysterious power that holds us in a particular way when we find the courage to risk, or when we give ourselves to a life that is more challenging and demanding than we have previously known. We seek this experience in many exciting ways: in the newness of a moment that pushes our comfortable edges, in fashions and trends, or in something dangerous like mountain climbing. It doesn't matter. We look for anything that makes us feel unheld, if only for one risky moment. Unheld by the collective and personal *known*. We want to be out on a limb, out of the range of human control. We want to feel the thrill of going forward against the odds, risking it all, and surviving gloriously! We bring the mystery of this survival back to the tribe as a story—a precious gift to be shared, ritualized, and handed on to those not yet born. We want these myths to help the tribe survive the challenges of an unimaginable future.

My own story was still forming, and I was not sure if I would make it back to the tribe safely to tell it. I was not completely certain that I hadn't abandoned my tribe altogether when I leapt into unknown formlessness. I knew my tribe of fellow artists was threatened by my decision to destroy my art. Perhaps I was to discover a new tribe, a creative or spiritual order that I could give myself to. But I did not know how to choose such an order. If I were to find a new art form or seek out a religious tradition, how would I do that and what would it look like? I trusted that such things were up to God, yet secretly hoped that something might divinely choose me. I longed for a way to justify my strange relationship to the vastness that surrounded me. I had read many spiritual and religious books and was deeply moved by what seemed to be the essential truths common to various religious practices. If, in fact, one God was running the show, then I could not change anything significant by relieving myself of the burden of my personal interface with formlessness and taking on just another variety of worship. Worship of any other form was essentially the same as the path I had just abandoned—the worship of art.

As a spiritual path, art carried my life as far as it could within the limited scope of determined human effort and discipline. I knew I could not have given one more ounce of myself to art as worship and have survived. In retrospect, I honestly believe that my survival was at stake—certainly survival of the spirit, perhaps of the body as well. Ramakrishna has a wonderful parable about the vehicle of one's particular discipline. It goes something like this: When you take a boat across a river and you reach the other side, you do not drag the boat with you beyond that point.

I came to understand what the generations of artists preceding me had come up against: a point when the abstract, the conceptual, and perhaps even the formless presented itself as the spirit of their time. When we see nineteenth- and twentieth-century art from the perspective of the twenty-first century, we apprehend that the golden thread moving through art history is making its way toward heaven.

First, the Impressionists released art from its sentimental fix on the literal, material world. With great courage, they explored what was formless and energetic behind the perfect depictions of flesh and bone. Next in art's heaven-bound progression came the exploration of the abstract and surreal dimensions. These artists trusted the approach to heaven by dabbling in the area of malleable spirits. Theirs was the disembodied human experience of the dreamscape. They blended open, fluid forms with solid, physical reality, inching their way a little closer toward heaven's gates.

Marcel Duchamp? He fits in somewhere and everywhere. He is a bodhisattva who knows no bounds. He was probably the first hungry shaman to invoke an antelope by ceremonially painting it on the cave wall. With great precision, he mischievously juggled art and magic, from the beginning of time no doubt. I am certain that, as an artist, he incarnates eternally, showing us how it is *really* done.

Jackson Pollock danced with the powerful energies of his raw, naked experience of art. He imploded—splattering and flying right over the wall, setting art down in an unexpected proximity to heaven. Bones dripping, he danced to the music of the universe. He trusted wildly, doubted, and died of exposure. Mark Rothko, too—veins slit and D.O.A., bleeding ever so softly into the canvas.

Then the wanderings of the conceptual artists. Impressively, they drove with no hands on the wheel, but they went more wide than deep. Nonetheless, their outrageous courage delivered art a little closer to a vast and formless heaven. Pop artists abandoned the direct pursuit of heaven altogether; instead, they indulged in the things that distract us from heaven, while simultaneously pointing them out as obstacles. Andy Warhol was the undisputed, flagrant King of Pop. No one will ever again get away with what he did. His preeminent position as the royal child of art assured complete forgiveness. Unhindered, with dominion over the material world, he took the best seat in the house, brought in all his friends, and then ravaged the place. His was truly a creative act of power, and America, seeking to justify its greed, hardly even noticed his mischievous smile.

Many of the truly great artists of the forties, fifties, and sixties, who so beautifully created the new expressions and explored the difficult spiritual terrain of formlessness, did not seem to survive their encounters very well. They skirted the formless black hole, and the best of them seemed to get pulled in and consumed by its gravitational pull.

There has to be a way, within the search itself, to survive the encounter. Within their limited control, physical and mental creation cannot contain a complete enough awareness to allow the artist the full experience of the blast of formlessness. What if we were to align ourselves with the calm center of formlessness and dive right down the middle? Where would we come out, if indeed we came out at all? Creation obviously is pulling us in this direction. There must be an overlooked or unexplored larger dimension that can carry creation past the threshold of human expression, past the metaphoric death of form, and into a self-maintaining heaven where one can survive the creative formless encounter.

In my own exploration, I saw that what I had available as a human being and an artist was not enough. I needed a quantum leap, through a force larger than my own, to break my stalemate with formlessness. The final victory of this journey had to be so complete as to deliver *all of life* onto the solid ground of a sustainable new vision. Discovering this anew is, I believe, the terrifying and impossible task of the artists of each generation.

My immediate paradoxical stalemate was this: When form was in place, life felt like death, but so did trusting in a life that seemed to be an impossible vacuum. I experienced this vacuum in a very literal sense. It was all that was left after I gave away everything and abandoned my form of creative expression. This unresolved paradox left me open to a new spiritual form that might guide my life into an inhabitable atmosphere. Not knowing quite what to do to find this form, I stayed creatively open to all possibilities. I thought that perhaps I could enter a religious order if one were to naturally present itself. Wherever it took me, the allure would have to be that of courage rather than the fearful avoidance of formlessness. Courage was all I knew to use as a guidepost.

Willing Participants in the Unfolding

A mature creative life, which has discovered its source, finds it is linked to *everything*. When we are able to tap this source and link the illumined threads, we no longer want to live our creative lives separate from it. A creation that does not have the residual glow of its source can, at best, only sound a deathly rattle—however impressive that rattle may be.

In my own exploration, I found that my very identity as an artist became too limiting for the expanding, creative universe I was discovering. By limiting my focus only to the creation of art, I inadvertently held at bay art's potential conscious link to everything. Hovering expectantly while doing the most mundane of activities, might just as effectively illumine creation. If we hold all aspects of our lives in unknowing, with equal attention, something may surprise us and become the unexpected entrance into a magical new encounter.

By taking responsibility for what is manageable in our lives and tending the small things with reverence, we can relinquish the impossible attempt to play god to our larger creation. There is great freedom in knowing that nothing is ours to hold or identify with. Any victory or accomplishment gets offered back, brightening the overall light of a vaster whole. In the brightening, creativity becomes more detached. We place it in the service of a mystery that we can then join forces with. In this scenario, attentively refraining from interfering with the mystery becomes far more useful an activity than any strategic involvement. Properly invited, the mystery becomes the well-prepared, *empty* channel through which inspiration can enter.

Creation actually requires very little, too little for most of us to handle. There is not much in our postmodern, western culture that teaches us to pay attention to the things that require less. These things give birth to the unpredictable surprises that inspire a larger and deeper soul connection with creative life. With the soul well tended, even when all is lost (which it inevitably is in death), our creation lives larger than its physical limits.

The best that any of us can do with the heaven and hell that surrounds us is to become willing participants in the unfolding of our soul's life. Any creative act emerging from this tending becomes One with the elements of the Mystery.

THE INSPIRED HEART

The most complete expression of the zeitgeist by art in my generation is best described as one of *wholeness*. Art, full circle, is the human story. In this story, metaphoric death is inevitable, and the consciously lived life offers the possibility of something new. A Hindu mystic said, "To set out with any holy purpose and to 'die' along the way is to succeed." High Art is the gift of resurrection as we continually die along the way. It is the Master's piece, a surrender into the hands of a success larger than our own. We may need to pass through the darkness as a prerequisite to completion, but as in birth, darkness is forgotten when the new life presents itself. Our completed circle becomes a container that represents a dimension larger than we originally anticipated. It can hold life—our own and others. We cannot know this by maintaining a safe intellectual distance from the full experience of the journey. We must give ourselves to the experience creatively, completely, and with consistent attention.

As small human beings, we must believe in something with all our heart and soul, even if what we believe in turns out to be a false god. The god that "fails" may, in fact, hold the seed of our success if we trust our original good and innocent intention. What is faith if it does not hold up, however hesitantly, in the face of apparent death? The very place the world seems to fail is the same place where intelligence, will, and good intentions no longer work for us. They may actually become destructive forces should we push beyond their limited capacity to be useful tools in our lives.

Most artists believe (however unconsciously) that they can create their way to heaven. This is a good and noble ambition but impossible to achieve. Paradoxically, to do anything less than to try to create a heaven on earth is to waste a perfectly good life. The belief that we can do what has never been done moves hope into action. Forces larger than our efforts can accomplish our dream, but we cannot avoid the moment of failure, in which we must rely on those forces. Our innocent, passionate belief in the possibilities inherent in this world, in spite of our apparent human limitations, lets God know we mean business! Great art comes out of this quest.

Yet, it is not enough to simply know this truth. Many scholars can speak eloquently on this subject, and in a sense, they know *about* this truth. But only in the moment of real surrender—a moment when that which is known no longer holds—are we given the pure, simple experience of the arrival of something holy, which is ancient and yet truly new, in the best and most inspired sense of the word. To go beyond the limits of human effort through surrender is to go beyond death.

I spoke in an earlier chapter about artists who came up against this moment in the fifties and sixties and about many of their untimely deaths, some deliberate, some perhaps not. I believe that those who destroyed themselves arrived at their metaphorical death and could go no further. They could not assimilate the full blast of their encounters with the energetic conditions of the formless abstract. The ego's identity with form and control had to be relinquished. This relinquishing is often more difficult than physical death itself. We need only look at the fear-based choices many of us make and see the lives created out of those choices to know that this is true. Many of these self-destructive artists may have come to believe, consciously or unconsciously, that suicide was the inevitable alternative to surviving the death of the ego. I don't know. For whatever reason, many of us struggle enormously with this personal dilemma when confronted with the conditions and full blast of a radically inspired moment. We all have to face it at some point in our lives. The bottom line is that metaphorical death leads to either physical death or renewal. How we face this dilemma seems to have everything to do with the courage and freedom we are able to envision for ourselves. When we can allow the ego to die, we give ourselves to a mysterious quantum leap that takes us over the limits of death and into the territory of renewal.

Artists and mystics are often the first to discover beautiful new directions in consciousness. That these new directions inevitably take us through our worst fears is the reason most of us avoid the landscape completely. This is also why so many of the men and women who are the first to point the way for us—the bushwhackers of consciousness—have been misunderstood, condemned, or worse, killed. Death will always look like death even if it is only the death of a way of life that is no longer working for us, personally or collectively. It seems to me that our collective consciousness is up against that moment in which new expression and healthy change demand our attention.

What are we going to do? What are the artists seeing now? What are the choices that will allow us to die along the way and to succeed in our quest? The alternative to metaphoric death can only be fear or continued self-destructive behavior. There are no limits to the ego's manipulations and strategies as it attempts to dominate and control, even if it means destroying ourselves or our world. Like the artists of the fifties and sixties, we find that allowing our bodies to die is often much easier than allowing the well-established, rooted ideas about ourselves to die. How do we allow for the organic unfolding of the deeply spiritual, creative life that is our birthright?

We may find temporary rest in beauty itself, but with art, as with all other disciplines, the only territories consistently worth exploring are the badlands of limitation and fear. Creative life can only gain power and offer freedom as it moves forward in these areas. To journey onward across the holy ground of personally perceived limitation, and then to live out in determined beauty the mystery and the creation that awaits us at the end of that journey, is art, and life, at its very best. The particular form of expression an individual artist adopts while moving through this landscape is their unique gift, a natural by-product of a life well lived.

When the gift of the inspired heart is given, there is no longer a separation between art and any other aspect of our lives. We come full circle when we are fully and equally attentive to everything in our lives. There can be no identified, fixed priority, only the requirements of each given moment. We can no longer say, "I am an artist" or "I am a theologian" or "I am an anything" separate from the alluring Whole of the heart's inspiration, with all of its possibilities intact.

Everything counts and fits into place. The way we get out of bed in the morning becomes as important as the moment of creating an inspired new work of art. When we fix our gaze abstractly on the Whole, all action and nonaction have the potential to support what is holy and creative. High Art becomes the art of all things, of whispers from God in all directions. Creative life requires one to listen carefully to the whispers and to become fully involved in manifesting the products of a generous universe in the world. Art is as good a way as any to express the whisper, yet art is not defined as separate from any other expression of creation. What is important is not the particular form of creation, but the completed circle as the premise for right action in our world. We begin to see the patterns that connect our actions to those of others, centered in their own unique circles. The universal circle that emerges as we interconnect is the creative energy that holds our world in its new form. We become, with those we are connected to, the inspired heart of creation itself.

A Return to the New

When I stopped making art, I thought I would never go back to it again. I simply let it go. The film made about my art and life in 1979 was just being finished when I destroyed my art. The film was in the world on its own, separate from any further involvement on my part, so I had nothing more to do with it or with art. However, I still believed in the powerful potential of genuine, timely breakthroughs in art. I was simply at a point where my own artistic experience left completely, and I was done with art as an egoistic expression in the world.

I was certain that I had settled into a larger, all-inclusive, formless creativity, a form of exploration that I felt more alive in. I simply felt free of art as I had known it. Doing or not doing art was now all the same. Art held equal status with any of the other choices that a newly presented moment might offer. Interestingly enough, now that I was detached from it, the physical creation of art could reenter my life. At first it happened in small ways.

I remember the moment that I realized in a simple and newly conscious way that I was physically making art again. While walking down the street, I found a blank stamped envelope lying on the sidewalk and I picked it up. It had a piece of paper inside, so I thought I would write a letter to someone I had been thinking about. The stamp on the envelope was the head of someone important. I decided to draw a body to go with the head. Then I surrounded the body with an environment, which eventually became an entire scene. This simple act as an artist was a small seed, a rebirth of sorts. I knew that as long as I stayed in touch with this simplicity, then making art was just another healthy, creative way to dance with the angels, touching the physical world with aspects of that dance. I was familiar with this dance; it was a skill I had abandoned, yet it was fully developed, idling, and available. I find that the gods are very efficient beings. No aspect of life that we have invested with our hopes, dreams, and loving attention is wasted in the end. When we can release the personal identity that we so often impose on our chosen paths, and can give our gift into the hands of an alchemical process larger than our own, then our gift will be sanctified and returned. It will ultimately become infused with renewed life and power in the world. There is a wonderful Zen saying, "Die while alive and be completely dead, then do what you will. All will be good."

The tiny act of drawing on the found envelope was the beginning of creation's return flight into my life, sanctified. I was *doing what I wanted to do* in a new way. Since art was what I knew best, I brought it with me as a gift when I went somewhere to work with people, or when I stayed at someone's home. The offering of this aspect of my life was not any sort of barter, a word people often use in trying to explain my life. Instead, it was a spontaneous act with no strings attached, done out of love. When I created art for someone, it was the natural, immediate response to the calling of a larger harmony. Response of this type and nonattachment seem to be prerequisites for the sacredness and magic of any real offering to God or human.

There are stories of Eskimos [in Canada, known as Inuit] who spontaneously carved small ritual objects out of bone or antler. They carried their creations in their pockets, then left them behind or dropped them on the ground as they made their way to new territory, where they made new offerings to different spirits. The creative process, perhaps more than the objects themselves, served to empower their circumstances as they made their nomadic way to unexplored territory. The artifacts we see in museums are the mysterious offerings along the way to unseen demons, gods, and goddesses. They are the spent shells and arrowheads—all that remain of the powerful mythic battles fought for heaven and earth. They are evidence of lives lived fully in the spirit and in the requirements of the moment's calling. The right and creative use of matter is to fully empower the living experience and to create objects of beauty in the service of enormously demanding mythic dimensions.

It is easy to indulge in the luxury of thinking that we have so many choices available to us when we decide what to do with our lives. Yet to be fully alive is to have both feet on the ground in the badlands of *no choice*. In this land, no deals are made; we simply make offerings and talk to God, even about little things.

DOING OUR OWN WORK FIRST

Before I came to the island, I trusted my unusual path, but I did not understand how the life I lived would be of service in the mainstream culture. In my journey, I came to terms with the mythic dimensions of my path. When something in our lives initiates this mythic journey, we tend to take it personally, because of the very real difficulty involved in letting go of that which we see as our life. To my surprise, I can now use what I discovered from that transpersonal point of view to help others. Now my move to Whidbey Island makes sense to me in relation to the "death process" I surrendered to in 1979.

This is the work we all must do before we can be of service in our world. A saying by Lao Tzu goes something like this: First, we must do our own personal work, then we tend the necessary work of our family, then our community, then our world—in that order. Most of us go about that process quite backward, first jumping into the world and bringing our messy, unresolved issues with us. The attempt to do anything significant in the world before we have been deeply changed ourselves is a way to avoid real change. Good intention counts for very little in the mythic journey. Doing our own work *first* leads to our true and unique participation in the world we wish to serve.

We all change together in ways that are not under our control. We cannot know the outcome of the difficult work we are required to do. We simply have to trust the process. What we can unconditionally trust about change is that ultimately beauty creates beauty. However beautifully we can stand alone in what feels like death is how beautifully we stand in the new life. Our courageous stance in the face of death creates integrity in its truest sense. We cannot impersonate true integrity.

Once a larger shift has taken place, we choose as individuals whether we will accept and fully turn into the change at hand. The longer we avoid the holy process of real spiritual renewal, the more we suffer uselessly. This is true both personally and collectively.

What is the whispering message of divine law trying to tell us? Once we arrive at the answer to this question within ourselves, we can direct the journey of our world toward a beautiful, collective reality. The gods do, indeed, whisper before they scream. The only real power we have to eliminate useless suffering in our world is to remain attentive, as in prayer, to the whispers instructing our choices. The challenge for all of us in the West is to hear the quiet instructions first, and then to maintain that listening in a screaming, material world. Deep listening is a fearless, creative response worth cultivating above all else. It is creation's priceless pearl, which can roll with us through the inevitable deathlike experience and deliver us back into effective life in the world.

There is evidence of this listening! Artists and other sensitive listeners among us are usually the receptors of subtle change. They hear the whispers first. There are many indicators of a conscious golden thread running through the emerging culture. I am most familiar with the thread of light revealed by art history. True creative expression, seen as a series of consecutive art movements, is like the trail of a star as it shoots across the sky. It is meaningful creation written in light, evidence of something luminous and largely aware, moving across time. Creativity brings into form inspired, new reality. Perceived from a retrospective vantage point, art history is simply an evolving series of divinely inspired whispers arranged neatly in a row. Intuition of the language of the stars is given to anyone fearlessly willing to let go of the past and to open themselves to the emerging forces of the divine.

Literal creative expression is secondary. The most direct manifestation of inspired creative breakthrough may very well be the blast of formless direct experience alone. In a creative moment of earth-shattering awe, emptiness paints its final masterpiece in starlight. Artistic expression can only offer a hint of this direct experience.

When we have experienced the mythic dimension underlying all of matter, we are then able to link it to the creative life going on around us. A receptor of the whispering star trail, Dorothy Fadiman (the visionary filmmaker) had an interesting insight into the transpersonal dimension of my own small encounter.

A few years ago, Dorothy visited us. She watched the film that was made about my art and life in 1979, which has now been incorporated into the 2001 Parabola video. The film ends with me talking about destroying my artwork, letting go of my worldly life, and in essence, leaping into the void, which for me, is the ultimate creative act. After watching the film, Dorothy sat silently for a long time, and then she turned to me slowly and asked, "When exactly did you do that?" I said, "In September of 1979." She became very quiet again, then lit up and said, "I felt *exactly* when that shift happened in art too."

This is not *my* story; it is *our* story. If it is genuine, my success in grappling with the whispers of the terrifying void is our success, and yours in listening to your own whispers is mine. So basically, who can claim as their own the big bang of an evolving story that belongs to all of us? We do, however, each have an essential part to play, and that part is usually more than most of us can accomplish in one lifetime. However, the conditions of this time offer us an especially good possibility to fulfill our part. I believe that this is a holy time, in which conscious participation in our own full awakening is very possible.[2]

Cinema
Journey to the Source—Decoding *The Matrix Trilogy*

Pradheep Chhalliyil

The only incomprehensible thing about this universe is that it is comprehensible.

—Albert Einstein

In this chapter, Pradheep Chhalliyil first explains the plot of the film *The Matrix,* which is the first film of *The Matrix Trilogy.* (The other two are *The Matrix Reloaded* and *The Matrix Revolutions.*) Then, descriptions of selected scenes in the film are followed by Chhalliyil's commentary, in which he explains the movie from the perspective of the nondual teaching of the Upanishads. The scenes selected are key to understanding *The Matrix* and the entire trilogy.

THE PLOT OF *The Matrix*

The Matrix Trilogy explores the complex relationship between physical human beings and their perception of reality as controlled by a gigantic computer program. The story begins in the year 2199. Computers with advanced artificial intelligence (AI) have taken control of human life on the planet. These machines draw their power from the bio-chemical activity of thousands of human beings held captive inside capsule-like bubbles that feed them intravenous nutrients from birth to death. By plugging the humans' brains into a computer-simulated world, the machines prevent the humans from knowing the truth that they are being used as energy fuels. The computer-simulated world is called The Matrix.

All the sleeping human bodies incubated in the capsules are connected to this Matrix-generating computer via an implant in the back of their neck leading to their brains. Since all the brains are connected to one mainframe computer, each person perceives the same simulated world. The central computer feeds a continuous stream of stimuli to the brain causing each individual to perceive a full range of emotions and experiences associated with growing up, working, growing old, and finally dying. The inert humans live their whole life in a state of suspended animation, engaged in the computer-simulated Matrix world as if watching a movie. But in this case the simulation is so convincing that they feel they are actually living "real" lives.

The deception is so effective because the Matrix program creates a complete 3-D virtual world—parks, gardens, restaurants, offices, train stations, etc.—that people can experience exactly as if they were physically present. Interactions with other individuals are also programmed into this computer-generated reality, so that everyone lives in a fully plausible, common dream world, even though they are, in fact, lined up in row upon row of incubators in a huge storage area. They live their lives in total belief of the world that is generated for them by the computer.

Soon after The Matrix was first created, several individuals, led by one man, Morpheus (Laurence Fishburne), escaped from the illusory world of The Matrix and established their own colony in the underground City of Zion. Here they have their own computers through which they are able to hack into the Matrix program. These chosen few carry permanent "connector" holes in the back of their necks. By inserting a needle-like device into this hole they can be connected both to The Matrix and to the Zion computers, from which any physical ability, including boxing, flying helicopters, and kung fu, can be programmed into their brains. When connected to The Matrix, their physical bodies remain in Zion, connected to the Zion computers, much like the other humans in The Matrix stay in their incubators. The crucial difference, however, between the free humans and the captive humans is that the former can actually exit from The Matrix any time, as well detach themselves from the Zion computers. When separated from the computers they can live and perceive in normal reality. These free humans transport themselves in and out of The Matrix, where they use their specially downloaded mental and physical abilities to accomplish impossible feats, such as jumping hundreds of yards or dodging bullets by running up walls.

The main objective of the free humans is to destroy The Matrix by gaining enough understanding to break its code. The challenge, however, is not only to decode The Matrix, but also to prevent enemies, referred to as "agents," from entering The Matrix. The founder of The Matrix has created The Agents to protect the system. The Agents are able to transform themselves in and out of anybody's body, making them very difficult to eliminate. They do not die if shot in the head or pushed under a train. Instead, they simply leave the dead body and enter into another living one. However, despite The Agents' superhuman capabilities, they still live in a world based on rules. Because of this they are, in a sense, mortal, and in their mortality lies the hope to save mankind from The Matrix. For transportation the free humans use a hovercraft named The Nebudchadnezzar in which they travel throughout the sewers of old cities, pursued by killing machines called The Sentinels, robot killers also designed to seek and destroy free humans.

Within this complex environment is woven a fantasy tale of heroism and love. Morpheus has identified a young computer hacker called Neo (Keanu Reeves) as "The One" foretold by prophecy, who will destroy The Matrix and free mankind from slavery. Morpheus sends a female (free human), Trinity (Carrie-Anne Moss), into The Matrix to contact Neo and convince him of his destiny. Neo is given the choice to know the truth about The Matrix or to continue to live in ignorance like his fellow human beings. He chooses the former and takes a special red pill that unplugs him from The Matrix world. He is detached from the Matrix computer, removed from the incubators, and taken to Zion where his degenerated body can be rejuvenated. Neo, like the other free humans, can now connect to the Zion computers and enter and exit from The Matrix at will.

Morpheus shows Neo how all his previous perceptions are false and have been guided by The Matrix, thereby freeing his mind to discover his true identity and the part he must play in saving the world. It is not an easy task for Neo to regain his faculties of independent thinking. A double agent named Cypher (Joe Pantoliano) tries to persuade him to return to The Matrix and later on helps the agents to capture Neo's mentor, Morpheus.

Because Neo does not believe that he is The One to save Zion, Morpheus takes Neo to see The Oracle (Gloria Foster), a deceptively ordinary-looking old lady who is in fact a great seer, able to predict the future. She forces Neo to face his own self-doubts and grasp hold of the truth about himself, accept Trinity's love, and take his rightful place in the cosmic drama unfolding around him.

The film ends with Neo meeting his nemesis, Agent Smith (Hugo Weaving), as he attempts to free Morpheus from captivity. Agent Smith delivers a fatal bullet wound to Neo, but Trinity restores him to life with her love. Finally, beginning to trust his power, Neo is able to perceive Agent Smith as part of The Matrix. He penetrates the illusion of Smith's body and shatters him to pieces.

THE MATRIX WORLD

The wisdom of Enlightenment is inherent in every one of us. It is because of the delusion under which our mind works that we fail to realize it ourselves, and we seek the advice and guidance of enlightened ones.

—Hui-neng

The dialogue continues between Morpheus and Neo about the strange new world that Neo finds himself in.

When we look at the stars most of us can't help but wonder about the nature of the universe. From a scientific point of view we know these are physical bodies, but how and why are they dangling out there? Who put them there? We may think, "In this vastness of space and time, I am born and die, but is that the end of me? Do I vanish into nothing afterwards? Where was I before I was born?" Most of us cannot imagine that we will vanish forever. Something about this feels wrong, but we cannot explain exactly what. This constant wondering can drive us mad and it may eventually lead us to a teacher who claims to know the answer. Like all of us, Neo wants to know the Truth about the only world he has known so far, The Matrix.

Neo asks Morpheus to describe The Matrix. Morpheus tells him that The Matrix is so convincing that it prevents him from knowing the Truth about the world.

Morpheus says this Matrix world is not real. It is created to look so real that everyone is convinced they are living a real life: going to work, watching television, paying taxes, going to church, etc. But it is a trick. The Matrix world is created to be so real that no one will ever know the truth about who they are.

Morpheus gives Neo the shocking truth that he is a slave in the Matrix world.

Slave to whom? Naturally, like Neo, we don't feel that we are enslaved. We feel free to think and do whatever we desire in this world, free from anyone's influence. In the Matrix world the machines keep all the humans captive and use them as a source of energy. At the same time, in order to prevent them from knowing this truth, their minds are given a simulated version of life, in which they can be a doctor, an engineer, a lawyer, or an actor, pay taxes, go swimming, eat pizza, have sex, visit Disneyland, spend holidays in Hawaii, etc. Their world is only a computer-generated projection of the mind. What about us? Even if we buy the idea that the world we experience is just a projection of our mind as in The Matrix, we still feel it is in our control. So the million dollar question is: Do we have control over our minds?

What Is Mind?

Thought can be defined as our capacity to be aware of something, subjective or objective. Awareness of anything is thought. The physical organ which facilitates the manifestation of these thoughts is the brain, while the constant flow of thoughts is called the mind. Our identity is based on the thoughts we have in our minds. The body is made of thirty trillion cells, but all are controlled by the mind. You want to eat, you open your mouth. You want to walk, your legs start moving. The person who controls all of this, we think of as "I" or "Me." But according to the Upanishads, even the "I" is a concept, a thought like any other. Exactly like the humans in The Matrix, we think we have a life, but in fact it is all conjured up by the mind or Maya.

As long as we are plugged into our Matrix-like world we have the "I" thought with a definite body and mind sense complex. The irony is that we think we control our thoughts, but in reality our thoughts control us. Our mind dictates our every experience fed by the senses, from taste to smell, touch, and other sensual pleasures.

Most of the time we act the way the mind wants to: "'I' did this or that, because 'I' thought it was right."

Because every thought depends on the mind—the thinker—we become a slave to the mind. Every experience we go through, every impression we take-in molds our future thoughts and actions. As we go through life we program ourselves to accept a world that is not more real than the world of The Matrix. Our world becomes a Self-created reality with its own mind-created logic to justify it. Thus we lose our real freedom, our unbounded nature. If "happy" thoughts flow, we are happy. If "sad" thoughts flow, we are sad. All emotions are nothing but thoughts. If they get completely out of control we can even go insane. And it all seems so real!

The truth is that the mind and the world it creates for us come from and are sustained by our own Source or Self. But we get so caught up in the game of life that we lose sight of it, like a child playing a video game in an arcade and forgetting to go home.

The Mind Machine

The "mind machine" is what controls our world, exactly like the Matrix computer controls the humans in the movie. The machines in the Matrix world use human energy as a source of fuel. In our Matrix-like world also, the mind feeds on the energy of the body to play its games. As long as we remain ignorant of this, we stay equally in bondage to our mind and senses as the people in the movie.

Is this truth or fiction? Let's take a look at a scientific perspective. According to the biochemistry of the body, a substantial part of our energy goes into supporting the thinking process. Everything is controlled from the brain, which needs maximum nutrition. The fuel for the brain is glucose. Through the process of digestion and biochemical processing, food is converted to glucose for transmission to the brain via the blood stream. Even if the body is starved of food, stored fats are accessed to maintain the supply of glucose to satisfy the brain, the "king" of the body. The human brain is one of the most energy hungry organs in the body. Although the brain accounts for less than 2 percent of a person's weight, it consumes 20 percent of the body's energy and 20 percent of the total oxygen consumption, even at rest. While we are thinking (thoughts), the brain consumes energy at ten times the rate of the organs in the body. The glucose needed to feed our brain comes from plants, which access the sun's energy, and so Morpheus tells Neo that the machines evolved from using plants (Sun) to using human bodies as an energy source.

So we could say our thoughts use our body as an energy source. The thousands of Sentinels that attack Zion City in *Matrix Revolutions* are like the thoughts fighting for their own existence within The Matrix against the free humans who want to cut off their energy source. The only way to stop them is for Neo to go to The Source. Once he is there the thoughts naturally subside and go away, just as they do when the mind turns inside and meditates on the Self.

Morpheus tells Neo that everyone is a slave to the false world of The Matrix.

The prison of our mind is our false identifications with the world of the senses at the cost of knowing our soul or Self. When we are in the prison of the mind, we really believe whatever we want to believe, under its influence. Our wonderland, our life of misery and suffering, is the rabbit hole we dig with the narrow notions and relations of our mind. We make ourselves a slave to the mind and its limited potential, with our own notions.

When young elephants are captured in the forest, it is easy to tame their minds. The baby elephant is tied to a stake with a strong chain that it cannot break. Even when it grows into a mighty adult, easily able to break the chain, the elephant will not do so because its mind has become accustomed to not being able to break the chain. It is unable to set itself free from bondage even though it has greater physical strength. The conditioning becomes so strong that even when the chain is removed, the elephant will not try and escape.

Just like elephants, if we become prisoners of our own mental conditioning and are not taught to know our true identity, we live in the worst kind of bondage. The bondage is not outside. It is inside. Regular chains can be broken with physical force, but the bondage of the mind can only be removed through better understanding. And although a teacher can help show us the way, ultimately it is through our own effort that we must break the bonds of our ignorance. The Upanishads are very clear that liberation or Self-realization cannot be given by anyone else. Only the elephant can free itself from the notion that it cannot break the chain.

Morpheus tells Neo that The Matrix is not real but a trick of the mind.

The great teachers who have freed their minds from the Matrix-like world of thought-senses can guide us to be aware of the existence of our illusory world. But for us to really know about it, we have to see it ourselves. This is how material science differs from spiritual science. Spiritual science is subjective experience and cannot be shown to others. Each of us has to experience it directly. Like the illusory dream world, we have to wake up to know that the dream was not a reality.

The Blue or the Red Pill

Truth does not become error just because nobody believes it.

—Mahatma Gandhi

Morpheus places two pills in Neo's hand, one red and one blue. The blue one allows Neo to stay in the world of The Matrix; the red one allows him a chance to see Reality.

The *Katho Upanishad* says that, like Neo, everyone gets a choice in life. Either we take the path of Self-knowledge (*Sreyas*, the red pill) that leads us to the Truth, or we take the path of pleasure

(*Preyas*, the blue pill) that leads us to ignorance of our true nature. Those who choose the path of *Sreyas* will find happiness, while those who choose *Preyas* are destined to be deluded.

The red pill is a symbol of scriptural knowledge, such as the Upanishads. It is through the guidance of the scriptures that we can easily get unplugged from our Matrix-like world. These scriptures are not belief programs. They give us direct knowledge of our own true Self. Neo chooses the red pill and begins his journey of Self-discovery that will eventually lead him to The Source. The red pill is the symbol of that knowledge which removes darkness and spreads light. Hence in the East, saints and monks wear red and saffron-colored robes. Blue is the color of illusion or *Maya*. The "blueness" of the sky or ocean is not real but an illusion. In the Puranas, *Vishnu*, the maintainer of the creation, is known as a magician who casts illusion, and has blue skin. Only his outward appearance is blue, however. Inside, he is the manifestation of Truth (Pure Consciousness). This means that to know the Truth one has to transcend the veil of illusion of body-awareness.

Neo chooses the red pill. As he picks up the pill, two Neos are seen in the reflection of Morpheus' sunglasses, representing the two lives that Neo is leading. In the left lens we see the blue pill and Thomas Anderson [Neo's name in his Matrix life], and in the right lens we see the red pill and Neo.

Neo is taking the first step of Self-discovery. It is a journey he must ultimately make alone, but he needs a guide to help him. This is why learning the scriptures from a teacher who has many years of experience and reflection, allows us to tap into their deeper meanings.

Morpheus explains to Neo that the pill is a trace program to pinpoint his location.

The Upanishads teach that the Truth will only dawn on us when we disrupt the flow of thoughts that we are the body-mind-sense complex. If we think carefully, we don't know how to pinpoint our exact "location." We don't know who we really are. The wisdom of the Upanishads is like a trace program to point each of us towards the real "Me." How many of us are able to pinpoint exactly *Who am I?* and *Where am I? Am I in my head, or my heart, or my hand? Who exactly is Me?* In order to know this we have to disrupt the input and output of thoughts of the body-mind-complex. This is one of the first exercises that the Upanishads ask us to do. The discussion sessions between the master and the disciple are all about answering questions about the true nature of the Self. In the process they break the illusion, created by the mind, of who we are.

Cypher tells Neo that he will shortly be saying goodbye to The Matrix world.

Once we receive the true understanding about the reality of this world, we get "liberation" from the cycle of birth and death that we imagine ourselves to be in as part of our illusory world.

Neo sees a distorted mirror in front of him and is puzzled about how it came to be there.

He is puzzled to see his own reflection in the mirror and asks whether it is Morpheus who placed the mirror there. But before he gets an answer his reflection becomes clear in the mirror. He reaches out to touch it to see if it is real, but it melts like jelly on his fingers. He is not sure whether he is dreaming or not.

Morpheus asks Neo how he would know the difference between the world in his sleep and the world while he is awake.

This is the most important part of the movie because it helps us understand the illusory nature of The Matrix. Neo is confused. What is real and what is merely a reflection?

"The problem is that we think the world is 'outside' us when in reality the world is actually 'inside' us," says the spiritual teacher Vijay

Shankar. When we close our eyes at night the world completely disappears, only to magically reappear the next morning when we open our eyes again. So the world can be turned on and off like a computer monitor. The world is as much a projection of the mind as is the image on the computer screen a product of the software.

During sleep our whole identity disappears. In deep sleep we are not aware of anything at all. The *Upanishads* tell us that there is a fourth state of Consciousness, called *Thuriya*, which is beyond the states of waking, dreaming, or sleeping. In this "thoughtless" state we do not identify as being any one person in particular. This is our Self, our true unbounded nature. It is not a state of thinking, rather it is the source of all thoughts. In this state we know the difference between the dream and reality. It is a very blissful condition and the experience of it is the initial goal of all meditation techniques. From there we transcend to the state of "witnessing" our thoughts.

The dream state and the waking state are completely real experiences until we wake up from them. In a dream we can be chased by a tiger and run away in panic. Only when we fall out of bed and wake up do we realize that it was a dream. Only when we have a spiritual awakening do we realize that the seemingly solid physical world that we live in is also just a dream.

Neo Finds His True Self

The pill that Morpheus gives Neo is like the first exposure to the teachings of the scriptures (Upanishads). The essence of the Upanishads is *Tat-vam-asi*, meaning "You are THAT" (You and the Supreme soul or pure Consciousness are the same). The mirror first shows Neo his true Self as a perfect reflection, and then his Self appears distorted by the illusion of *Maya*. This distortion is caused by ignorance. The knowledge unfolded through the scriptures completely changes our perspective of the world to reveal our true Self. Whereas once we took ourselves to be the distorted image in the mirror, with proper knowledge we learn that we are different from the reflection. Neo finds this out as the mirror becomes him.

The mirror turns to fluid when Neo touches it and starts to spread over his entire body.

When we go to a hall of mirrors we laugh at our reflections in the different surfaces. In one we look like a dwarf, in another we are tall and thin, and in yet another we are fat. We don't feel upset about these twisted images of ourselves. We laugh. But in our supposedly real lives, instead of laughing at the reflections of our Self in bodies that are black, blonde, tall, short, thin, obese, ugly, and beautiful, we feel jealous or proud, angry or sad, insecure or pompous. If we knew the Truth, we would laugh at ourselves as much as we do in the hall of mirrors.

Neo cannot believe that what he sees is real.

At first, like Neo, we think this is strange. The truth is that what is odd is our ignorance of who we really are. Neo resists believing it. This is natural. The collective effect of our ignorance and past actions are so deeply ingrained in us that unreality appears real to us and truth loses its meaning. We keep on clinging to our sensory world even when the master shows us the Truth. We refuse to believe in it until we are completely "unplugged" from the sensory world.

The gel-like mirror sticks to Neo's finger and starts to spread all over his body and into his mouth.

Neo then finds himself caught in a web of wires, with a tube connected to his mouth. He pulls the tube out and spits the fluid out of his mouth. He struggles to get free from the web of wires and to break through the transparent membrane covering him. Immediately he sees millions of human beings individually encapsulated like chicken eggs in an incubator. A robotic machine grabs hold of his neck and immobilizes him. Neo sees his own face in a small lens that emerges from the machine. He looks bald and naked, innocent like a baby. The machine unplugs the steel probe from the back of his neck that has been feeding his brain with the computer-simulated Matrix world. As he is unplugged, the floor of the capsule opens up and Neo is washed out with the fluid.

This is a fabulous image of the world of bondage. Right from our conception in the womb we are caught in a web of control generated by our mind. Neo, in struggling to tear himself free from the transparent membrane, is throwing off the illusion (Maya) that covers his sight of his true Self. We don't suspect that we are encapsulated in the womb of Maya, just as none of the enslaved humans realize they are caught in The Matrix. It is the "red pill" of knowledge that reveals the illusion and "unplugs" us from it.

Unplugging from the Matrix World

> *The cuckoo bird drops her eggs in the crow's nest,*
> *The crow hatches it, nurses it, suspects nothing,*
> *Does not reject it and does not ask why.*
> *So does Maya, mother of creation perform this act in the womb.*
> —Tirumoolar in Thirumantiram (Verse 488)

We perceive the world the way our mind projects it. Like Neo, we are plugged into our Matrix-like world through the mind. When we unplug ourselves from our mind, we see our true Self, the soul. But the process of unplugging can be painful. The wires that are connected to Neo's body are similar to our senses; they can make us weak and a slave to our mind-projections. But that same thought process that plugs us into the illusion can also unplug us when it is led in the right direction by a spiritual teaching such as the Upanishads. As Neo is being unplugged, he sees his own reflection in the eyes of the machine that unplugs him. The whole process of plugging and unplugging is an act of his own Self.

However, without the conviction in the teachings, the transformation within us cannot occur. Then the Guru forces us into the training that Neo later undergoes. In this sense, the entire movie is about the struggle of a spiritual aspirant to recognize the Truth about himself and the efforts of his master to show it to him. At the end of the movie, conviction in the Truth finally makes Neo wake up from the dream world and see The Matrix world for what it is.

Neo's Spiritual Rebirth

He who planted seed, knew it not.
She who received saw it not.
The Creator knew, but He told none.
The Truth that reveals is also out there,
Yet I saw not Maya.
How cunning is her stealthy conduct!
—Tirumoolar in Thirumantiram (Verse 486)

After Neo is unplugged from the machine, he undergoes a second birth, his spiritual birth. This is beautifully illustrated when Neo slides naked like a baby through an apparent birth canal. He emerges like a newborn baby gasping for breath outside its mother's body. His disorientation is akin to the confusion of the spiritual aspirant when he first confronts the reality of the new world that his teacher has brought him to. The metal harness opens and drops the half-conscious Neo onto the floor of The Nebuchadnezzar where he finds himself looking straight up at the faces of Morpheus, Trinity, and Apoc.

Morpheus smiles and quietly tells Trinity that they have at last found the person they were looking for.

Part Five

Conclusion

Getting Self or God is not characteristic of the unfolding of the desire for nonduality. Recognizing Self or God is. Achieving Self or God is not characteristic of that unfolding. Understanding is. Being nondual isn't. Being is.

A strong awareness of things, persons, individual entities, remains. How can things appear so individualistic and be non-separate? The following chapters consider this question.

The Radical Nature of Nonduality

LET'S TAKE A LOOK AT SOME RADICAL DESCRIPTIONS OF NONDUALITY.

The Irish author who took the Asian name Wei Wu Wei describes nonduality as the "conceptual absence of 'neither Yes nor No'." "The 'Truth'," he says, "is the absolute absence of any kind of truth."[1]

In the Diamond Sutra, Buddha says, "all these molecules are not really such; they are called "molecules." [Furthermore,] a world is not really a world; it is [merely] called 'a world.'"[2]

Islam/Sufism: "If you think that to know Allah depends on your ridding yourself of yourself, then you are guilty of attributing partners to Him—the only unforgivable sin—because you are claiming that there is another existence besides Him, the All-Existent: that there is a you and a He."[3]

Judaism/Kabbalah: "Do not attribute duality to God. Let God be solely God. If you suppose that Ein Sof emanates until a certain point, and that from that point on is outside of it, you have dualized. God forbid! Realize, rather, that Ein Sof exists in each existent."[4]

What do these statements from major religions leave us with? Nothing. There is no you or I, they state—no world, no molecules, no essence or absence of essence—only Self, Allah, God, or Buddha. As Bernadette Roberts puts it, "[The] absolute nothing IS Christ."[5] It is Christ, Allah, God, Buddha, Self, the One, or whatever name resonates with your life.

These descriptions of the nature of nondual reality may seem uncomfortable. Maybe we do not "get" them. It may seem as though all the joy of living is sucked out by these descriptions, since there is no "you," no fun, or stuff to do. Bernadette Roberts said about the no-self condition or experience, which is the full understanding of the nature of nondual reality, that it is not "integrable with the human condition."[6]

The Heart Sutra and the Nature of Nonduality

THE HEART SUTRA INSTRUCTS US ON HOW TO VIEW THE NATURE OF things, of all existence, in relation to nonduality in its radical description.

Masanobu Fukuoka, known as the father of organic farming, resorts to the sutra:

> There is no east or west. The sun comes up in the east, sets in the west, but this is merely an astronomical observation. Knowing that you do not understand either east or west is closer to the truth. The fact is, no one knows where the sun comes from.
>
> Among the tens of thousands of scriptures, the one to be most grateful for, the one where all the important points are made, is the Heart Sutra. According to this sutra, "The Lord Buddha declared, 'Form is emptiness, emptiness is form. Matter and the spirit are one, but all is void. Man is not alive, is not dead, is unborn and undying, without old age and disease, without increase and without decrease.'"[1]

Wei Wu Wei explains the Heart Sutra:

"Form is emptiness," says the Heart Sutra (the Heart of the Prajna-paramita), "and emptiness is form." Then it explains: "Emptiness is nothing but form, and form is nothing but emptiness." Finally it completes the definition by adding: "Apart from emptiness there is not form, and apart from form there is no emptiness." In other words: "Apart from nothing there is no anything, and apart from anything there is no nothing." Or again, "Apart from our phenomenal world there is no Void, and apart from the Void there is no phenomenal world." The Void then is nothing, absolutely nothing—and Nothing is absolutely everything.[2]

Ibn 'Arabi reveals the wisdom within Sufism:

When the Prophet (peace and blessings be upon him) prayed and said:

> O my lord, show me the reality of things

what he meant by "things" was those things that appear to be other than Allah. He meant, "Teach me those things other than You. What is all this around me? Let me know. These things—are they You, or are they other than You? Did they exist before or did they come to be? Are they here forever or are they going to pass away?"

And Allah showed him that the "things" had no being and He showed "them" to be Him, and it was seen that all that appeared as other than Allah was His being. He was shown things without a name, without time, without quality, as the essence of Allah.[3]

In Kabbalistic Judaism we hear of beingness and nothingness:

> You may be asked, "How did God bring forth being from nothingness? Is there not an immense difference between being and nothingness?"
>
> Answer as follows: "Being is in nothingness in the mode of nothingness, and nothingness is in being in the mode of being." Nothingness is being and being is nothingness. The node of being as it begins to emerge from nothingness into existence is called faith. For the term "faith" applies neither to visible, comprehensible being, nor to nothingness, invisible and incomprehensible, but rather to the nexus of nothingness and being. Being does not stem from nothingness alone but rather, from being and nothingness together. All is one in the simplicity of absolute undifferentiation. Our limited mind cannot grasp or fathom this, for it joins infinity.[4]

In her revelatory style, with awesome beauty and insight into Christian scripture, Bernadette Roberts describes form and formlessness from the viewpoint of nondual Christianity. She says, "Like the resurrection the ascension reveals the inseparability of spirit and matter, the Formless and Form."

> Because consciousness or the mind cannot form any notion of the ascension, I wish to make clear that this particular experience is not a dissolving or disappearance of the body; it is not an out-of-the-body experience or the experience of a soul leaving the body. It was not an experience of bodilessness or the discovery of some other body and so on. Rather, it is the clear disclosure that the unknown substance of the physical body (Eternal Form or Christ's mystical body) dwells in a divine (heavenly or glorious) condition, which condition IS the unmanifest divine or Father. Thus where the resurrection reveals Christ as Eternal Form, the ascension reveals the unmanifest or Formless Father as the glorious condition in which Eternal Form dwells or exists. In itself a heavenly condition cannot

> be manifest, concretized or materialized; for this reason it always remains unmanifest. But the unmanifest is not all there IS to the divine; rather the unmanifest is eternally one with the manifest, which is why we say Christ is all that is manifest of the unmanifest. Too often we think that Christ was only "manifest" at the time of the incarnation, but the incarnation was only the revelation of the manifest divine. The divine manifest Christ is from all eternity; the incarnation was only the revelation of this Truth to man.
>
> The historical Christ never verbalized this great Truth (which nobody would have understood anyway), but silently demonstrated it with his resurrection and ascension. As we know, Christ's body dissolved into air, became invisible to the mind and senses, but what is this "air" into which Christ disappeared? This "air" is not only Christ's Eternal Form but the unmanifest condition (the Father) in which this Form eternally dwells. Like the resurrection the ascension reveals the inseparability of spirit and matter, the Formless and Form, which means that what man or consciousness does not know about spirit IS matter, and what he does not know about matter IS spirit; one is the mystery of the other.[5]

The practice of inquiry, the surrender of everything to Self or God, or merely instant direct seeing for no apparent reason, reveals what the Heart Sutra is saying. And the Heart Sutra tells us there is form and that form is us and all the things we do, all existence and every event and atom in existence, and that therefore it is all nothing even while everything is being done, playing out, being born, dying. Lex Hixon expresses how to live our lives out of this knowledge:

> To appreciate nonduality is not just sitting silently and thinking, or not thinking, but actively celebrating. Celebrating should be very human. That's why it's important to have delicious food, to make joyful conversation, to wear beautiful clothes. And it's a circle of nondual celebration,

which means that everyone must make a contribution to this celebration. Everyone without exception, to constitute a true circle, must celebrate the principle of nonduality, which is already functional within all awareness. We don't have to enter some other mystical state of consciousness.[6]

Things Stand Out Shining

THIS JOURNEY IN WHICH THE DESIRE FOR NONDUALITY PLAYS OUT IS not one in which longings, feelings, thoughts, emotions, personalities, and life activities end up blended into mush. The journey does not end up as a spirituality smoothie, cold and textureless.

The writings in this book are characterized by extraordinarily distinct places, people, and expressions. *So are our own lives.* How intensely, individually, and brightly do all things exist? Writing about the design of buildings, the architect and theorist Christopher Alexander speaks about a desire for not-separateness (nonduality) and how the formless—soul or spirit—is part of matter:

> Not-separateness, like everything else we have discussed, is a physical attribute of order. It is something which is visible in any building that has life. But when we concentrate on the problem of creating it, it arises only from a certain state of mind. Thus not-separateness simply means that a thing which is whole will be made, in the end, only by the genuine desire, on the part of the maker, not to be separate from the world. In other words, it is the state of mind of

the maker, in the end, which produces the deepest forms of order—and these deepest forms cannot be produced except by this state of mind. It requires the definite intention to become one with the world.

This idea cannot be realized in a building without a change, a quietness, in the maker. It requires absolute removal of the individual ego, because what is created can no longer stand out and be separated from everything else, and therefore loses its personal identity. And yet, paradoxically, in the moment where this absolute identity and not-separateness is attained in a thing, and it truly becomes one with the things which surround it, it stands out shining with an extraordinary power which could never be reached under any other circumstances. This is, perhaps, the central mystery of the universe: that as things become more unified, less separate, so also they become most individual, and most precious.[1]

A little more from Alexander:

A massive building or a small one, a seat, an ornament, a simple beam, a room, has life, is deep, affects us, moves us to tears, to awe, exactly to that extent that it is a picture of that God behind all things. If you see a watery pale yellow sunlight shining behind dark gray clouds, with the pale blue of heaven shining in between some wintery morning, and you see, in that light, the original light of the universe—then, you may say, in still different terms, that sometimes, very occasionally, an artist who weaves a carpet, or who shapes a building, or who paints a tile, manages to make something which has this same light in it, where this same Self is shining out . . . he has made something as close to a picture of God or Self as it can be, and it affects us, like the light of morning does, because it seems to show us directly to the heart of this self, and connects us with it, almost to the point of pain.[2]

The Worthwhile and the Impossible

MORIHEI UESHIBA, THE FOUNDER OF AIKIDO, GIVES US SOMETHING TO consider:

> Contemplate the workings of this world, listen to the words of the wise, and take all that is good as your own. With this as your base, open your own door to truth. Do not overlook the truth that is right before you. Study how water flows in a valley stream, smoothly and freely between the rocks. Also learn from holy books and wise people. Everything—even mountains, rivers, plants and trees—should be your teacher.[1]

The impossible cannot be spoken. Nor can we approach the impossible. When the *Avadhuta Gita* says, "There is no substance whatever which is of the nature of Reality," this expression sounds impossible to understand.[2] It is impossible to do anything to know that fully. We have to be "gone" to have that knowledge. The knowledge cannot be had.

We cannot do anything to achieve "goneness." However, we can take steps to achieve the worthwhile. The worthwhile is our sense of being, the taste of being, which gives us perspective that eases suffering. That is, we come to know ourselves as "being" rather than "being this" or "being that." From the worthwhile to the impossible, from form to formlessness, from thing to nothing, from the here to the gone, exists no bridge. They are not separate.

The desire for nonduality is the desire for the impossible and the discovery of the worthwhile. The teaching of nonduality says the worthwhile and the impossible are not separate.

When we seriously consider this non-separate reality, our identity becomes muddled. The walls that define who we are become flimsy and disappear. All things are seen as they are, without the blockage or gauziness of walls. Things standing out shining.

One day, in front of an audience of a thousand monks and nuns, the Buddha held up a flower. For a long time he said nothing. Everyone was quiet. Some shifted their sitting position to reflect a change in mental positioning. Time passed. Some had gone to Oz. Others were playing their roles in the Matrix. No one could understand the meaning behind the Buddha's gesture of holding up a flower and remaining silent. Finally someone in the audience smiled. And the Buddha smiled.

Notes

Part One: What Is Nonduality?

1. The Wizard of Oz (1939). www.imdb.com/title/tt0032138/quotes.
2. Swami Ashokananda, translator, *Avadhuta Gita*. Mylapore, Madras: Sri Ramakrishna Math, 1988.
3. Beck, Charlotte Joko, *Everyday Zen: Love and Work*. New York: HarperCollins, 1989.
4. Herrigel, Eugen, *Zen in the Art of Archery*. New York: Vintage Books, 1989.
5. Ibid.
6. Wren-Lewis, John, "The Dazzling Dark," *What Is Enlightenment?*, 1995.

Part Two: Bhagavan Sri Ramana Maharshi

1. Godman, David, ed., *Be as You Are: The Teachings of Sri Ramana Maharshi*. London: Penguin Books, 1985.
2. All the quotes in this and the following two paragraphs are by Ramana Maharshi and are fully attributed in the following two chapters of this book.
3. This biographical material is adapted from the website www.realization.org.

The Essential Teachings: Bhagavan Sri Ramana Maharshi

1. Ramana Maharshi, *Maharshi's Gospel*. Tiruvannamalai, India: Sri Ramanasramam, 1994, pp. 28-9.
2. Venkatasubramanian, T.V.; Butler, Robert; and Godman, David, trans., *Padamalai*. Boulder, Colorado: Avadhuta Foundation, 2004, pp. 187, 189.

3. Ramana Maharshi, *The Collected Works of Sri Ramana Maharshi*. Tiruvannamalai, India: Sri Ramanasramam, 2002, p. 66.
4. Ibid., p. 69.
5. Ibid., pp. 73-4.
6. *Padamalai*, pp. 189-91.
7. *The Collected Works of Sri Ramana Maharshi*, p. 52.
8. Ibid., p. 55.
9. Ibid., pp. 55-6.
10. *Maharshi's Gospel*, pp. 15-16.
11. *Ibid.*, pp,. 24-5.
12. *Ibid.*, pp. 78-9.
13. *Sri Ramana Jnana Bodham*, vol. 8, verse 462, cited in *Padamalai*, p. 186.
14. *Maharshi's Gospel*, pp. 79-83. Some portions of the sequence have been omitted.
15. *Ibid.*, p. 85.
16. Sastri, Kapali, *Sat Darshana Bhashya*. Tiruvannamalai, India: Sri Ramanasramam, 1975, pp. iii-v.
17. Ibid., p. ix.
18. *The Collected Works of Sri Ramana Maharshi*, pp. 59, 61.
19. Ibid., p. 62.
20. *Maharshi's Gospel*, p. 39.
21. Ibid., pp. 16-17.

On Practice: Bhagavan Sri Ramana Maharshi

1. Venkatasubramanian, T.V.; Butler, Robert; and Godman, David, trans., *Padamalai*. Boulder, Colorado: Avadhuta Foundation, 2004, p. 201.
2. Ramana Maharshi, "Who Am I?," unpublished translation based on one by Sadhu Om and Michael James, and modified by David Godman.
3. Venkataramiah, Munagala S., ed., *Talks with Sri Ramana Maharshi*. Tiruvannamalai, India: Sri Ramanasramam, 1984, talk no. 29.
4. *Padamalai*, p. 200.
5. Brunton, Paul, *Conscious Immortality*. Tiruvannamalai, India: Sri Ramanasramam, 1984, p. 176.
6. *Padamalai*, p. 202.
7. *Talks with Sri Ramana Maharshi*, talk no. 222.

8. *Padamalai*, pp. 202-3.
9. *Talks with Sri Ramana Maharshi*, talk no. 390.
10. Ramana Maharshi, *Maharshi's Gospel*. Tiruvannamalai, India: Sri Ramanasramam, 1994, p. 77.
11. Mudaliar, A. Devaraja, *Day by Day with Bhagavan*. Tiruvannamalai, India: Sri Ramanasramam, 1977, 22nd March, 1946.
12. *Talks with Sri Ramana Maharshi*, talk no. 486.
13. *Padamalai*, p. 206.
14. Ramana Maharshi, *Truth Revealed*. Tiruvannamalai, India: Sri Ramanasramam, 1982, v. 30.
15. *Padamalai*, pp. 207-8.
16. *Talks with Sri Ramana Maharshi*, talk no. 28.
17. *Day by Day with Bhagavan,* 1st March, 1946.
18. *Padamalai*, p. 216.
19. *Talks with Sri Ramana Maharshi*, talk no. 208.
20. *Maharshi's Gospel*, pp. 22-3.
21. *Padamalai*, p. 217.
22. *Talks with Sri Ramana Maharshi*, talk no. 244.
23. *Day by Day with Bhagavan*, 1st March, 1946.
24. *Padamalai*, p. 218.
25. Muruganar, *Guru Vachaka Kovai* (Tamil). Tiruvannamalai, India: Sri Ramanasramam, 1998, v. 472, cited in *Padamalai*, p. 219.
26. *Talks with Sri Ramana Maharshi*, talk no. 450.

PART THREE: NONDUAL CONFESSTIONS

1. Wren-Lewis, John, "The Dazzling Dark," *What is Enlightenment?*, 1995.
2. Swami Ashokananda, translator, *Avadhuta Gita*. Mylapore, Madras: Sri Ramakrishna Math, 1988.
3. Ibid.
4. Ibid.
5. 'Arabi, Ibn, *Divine Governance of the Human Kingdom*. Louisville, KY: Fons Vitae, 1997.
6. Matt, Daniel C., *The Essential Kabbalah: The Heart of Jewish Mysticism*. New York: HarperSanFrancisco, 1995.

7. Lao Tzu, *Tao Te Ching: The Classic Book of Integrity and the Way*. New York: Bantam Books, 1990.
8. Ibid.
9. Nerburn, Kent, ed., *The Wisdom of the Native Americans*. Novato, CA: New World Library, 1999.
10. Ibid.
11. Roberts, Bernadette, *What Is Self?*. Boulder, CO: Sentient Publications, 2005.
12. Ibid.
13. Wei Wu Wei, *Ask the Awakened*. Boulder, CO: Sentient Publications, 2002.
14. *The Collected Works of Sri Ramana Maharshi*, pp. 59, 61.

Judaism: The Essential Kabbalah

1. *Encyclopædia Britannica*, 2005, s. v. "Kabbala."

Christianity: Steps in My Christian Passage

1. Earlier Roberts wrote about the smile of recognition as follows: "The day of dawning was the simple recognition that all form, or the void of voids, that remains beyond all self or consciousness, that form IS Christ. This dawning came about in what I have called a 'smile of recognition,' which, unfortunately, is not an apt description. There comes a point when anything we say is NOT it, because anything we say fails to convey absolute Truth."

PART FOUR: NONDUAL PERSPECTIVES

1. Prendergast, John J. , *The Sacred Mirror: Nondual Wisdom & Psychotherapy*. St. Paul, MN: Paragon House, 2003.
2. Harrison, Steven, *The Happy Child: Changing the Heart of Education*. Boulder, CO: Sentient Publications, 2002.
3. Wennstrom, Jerry, *The Inspired Heart: An Artist's Journey of Transformation*. Boulder, CO: Sentient Publications, 2002.
4. Chhalliyil, Pradheep, *Journey to the Source: Decoding Matrix Trilogy*. Fairfield, IA: Sakthi Books, 2004.

Psychotherapy: The Sacred Mirror

1. I wish to thank my coeditors Peter Fenner, Ph.D., and Sheila Krystal, Ph.D., for their valuable suggestions and feedback for this chapter.
2. For three excellent examples of this phenomenon, see Eckhart Tolle's *The Power of Now*, Byron Katie's *Loving What Is,* and Tony Parson's *As It Is.* Also see Lynn Marie Lumiere and John Win's *The Awakening West: Conversations with Today's New Western Spiritual Leaders.*
3. See David Loy's *Nonduality: A Study in Comparative Philosophy.*
4. Prendergast, John J., *The Sacred Mirror: Nondual Wisdom & Psychotherapy*. St. Paul, MN: Paragon House, 2003.

The Radical Nature of Nonduality

1. Wei Wu Wei, *Posthumous Pieces*. Boulder, CO: Sentient Publications, 2004.
2. Price, A.F., trans., *The Diamond Sutra & the Sutra of Hui-neng*. Boston: Shambhala, 1990.
3. 'Arabi, Ibn, *Divine Governance of the Human Kingdom*. Louisville, KY: Fons Vitae, 1997.
4. Matt, Daniel C., *The Essential Kabbalah: The Heart of Jewish Mysticism*. New York: HarperSanFrancisco, 1995.
5. Roberts, Bernadette, *What Is Self?*. Boulder, CO: Sentient Publications, 2005.
6. Ibid.

The Heart Sutra and the Nature of Nonduality

1. Fukuoka, Masanobu, *One-Straw Revolution: An Introduction to Natural Farming*. Goa, India: Other India Press, 2004.
2. Wei Wu Wei, *Ask the Awakened*. Boulder, CO: Sentient Publications, 2002.
3. 'Arabi, Ibn, *Divine Governance of the Human Kingdom*. Louisville, KY: Fons Vitae, 1997.
4. Matt, Daniel C., *The Essential Kabbalah: The Heart of Jewish Mysticism*. New York: HarperSanFrancisco, 1995.
5. Roberts, Bernadette, *What Is Self?*. Boulder, CO: Sentient Publications, 2005.
6. Lex Hixon, www.theconversation.org.

Things Stand Out Shining

1. Alexander, Christopher, *The Nature of Order: An Essay on the Art of Building and the Nature of the Universe, Book Four, The Luminous Ground*. Berkeley: The Center for Environmental Structure, 2004.
2. Ibid.

The Worthwhile and the Impossible

1. Ueshiba, Morihei, *The Art of Peace*. Boston: Shambhala, 2002.
2. Swami Ashokananda, translator, *Avadhuta Gita*. Mylapore, Madras: Sri Ramakrishna Math, 1988.

Acknowledgments

Susan Dane's editorial contributions crystallized the approach to take for this book. Connie Shaw understood and believed in the vision and shaped the book so that it would stand out shining. I am grateful to David Godman for his selection of writings for this book from works on Bhagavan Sri Ramana Maharshi.

Gloria Lee, Mark Otter, Christiana Duranczyk, Andrew Macnab, Michael Read, and John Metzger have been friends and long-time editors of the Nondual Highlights, a daily online publication out of which this book arose. I thank the people who joined me in 1998 to form Nonduality Salon, the first online community dedicated to nonduality, and all the members past and current. I am in awe of each one who had the courage to speak in the Salon. There have been too many participants to mention. The founders of Nonduality Salon and long time participants, in the order in which I recall meeting them, are "Gene Poole," Gloria Lee, David Hodges, Dr. Harsh K. Luthar, and Jan Barendrecht.

Gloria Lee, Kelly Weaver, Dustin LindenSmith, Cee Albert, Christiana Duranczyk contributed to this book through their encouragement, love, support, presence, steadfastness, and friendship over many years. Thanks to Mike Himelstein for thirty years of humor, wisdom, and extraordinary friendship, which influenced my work in the field of nonduality. I am deeply grateful for the encouragement and vision of my late wife Dolores who said time after time, in the days before the Internet, that I would be connecting with a number of people about the teaching of nonduality. The journey through the world of nonduality is young and we are all still together.

Permissions

Ask the Awakened, by Wei Wu Wei. Boulder, CO: Sentient Publications, 2002. Reprinted with permission.

Avadhuta Gita, by Swami Ashokananda, translator. Mylapore, Madras: Sri Ramakrishna Math, 1988. Reprinted with permission.

The Essential Kabbalah: The Heart of Jewish Mysticism, by Daniel C. Matt. New York: HarperSanFrancisco, 1995. Reprinted with permission.

The Essential Teachings: Bhagavan Ramana Maharshi, selections by David Godman, is an original piece. Printed with permission.

The Happy Child: Changing the Heart of Education, by Steven Harrison. Boulder, CO: Sentient, 2002. Reprinted with permission.

Hixon, Lex. www.theconversation.org. Reprinted with permission.

The Inspired Heart: An Artist's Journey of Transformation, by Jerry Wennstrom. Boulder, CO: Sentient, 2002. Reprinted with permission.

Journey to the Source: Decoding Matrix Trilogy, by Pradheep Chhalliyil. Fairfield, IA: Sakthi Books, 2004. Reprinted with permission.

The Nature of Order: An Essay on the Art of Building and the Nature of the Universe, Book Four, The Luminous Ground, by Christopher Alexander. Berkeley: The Center for Environmental Structure, 2004. Reprinted with permission.

The One Alone, by Ibn 'Arabi (Tosun Bayrak, interpreter) is excerpted from Divine Governance of the Human Kingdom, Louisville, KY: Fons Vitae, 1997. Reprinted with permission.

The Sacred Mirror: Nondual Wisdom & Psychotherapy, by John J. Prendergast. St. Paul, MN: Paragon House, 2003. Reprinted with permission.

On Practice: Bhagavan Ramana Maharshi, selections by David Godman, is an original piece. Printed with permission.

Tao Te Ching: The Classic Book of Integrity and The Way, by Lao Tzu, Victor H. Mair, translator. New York: Bantam Books, 1990. Reprinted with permission.

The Ways of the Spirit, by Ohiyesa. From *The Wisdom of the Native Americans,* Kent Nerburn, editor. Novato, CA: New World Library, 1999. Reprinted with permission.

What Is Self?, by Bernadette Roberts. Boulder, CO: Sentient, 2005. Reprinted with permission.

The Wisdom of the Native Americans, Kent Nerburn, editor. Novato, CA: New World Library, 1999. Reprinted with permission.

Index

abidance
  as egoless silence, 38
  as "I", 33
  in real truth, 108
  in Self, 17–18, 28
Absolute, the
  Christ as a further revelation of, 98
  defined, 90
  Self, 36, 49
  universe as nature of, 53
  See also Self; truth
Advaita Vedanta. See Avadhuta Gita
aham-vritti ("I"-thought). *See* "I"-thought (*aham-vritti*)
air. *See* "divine air"; inhalation
ajnani (unenlightened person), characteristics of, 21, 24, 25
Alexander, Christopher, 187–188
Allah
  can only see Himself, 58
  as first and last, 57
  has no partners, 60
  nothing can be done to know, 59, 62
  and things as not other than, 61
  and your non-existence, 59
  See also God; Ibn 'Arabi, biography of
appearances, delusion of, 108
architecture and nonduality, 187–188
aroma of infinity, 67
art
  and avoiding surrender, 152–153
  and becoming nothing, 144
  and creation, act of, 149–150
  and deep listening, 157
  and Duchamp, Marcel, as *bodhisattva*, 148
  and the Impressionists, 147
  and non-separation, 153–154, 187–188
  and Pollock, Jackson, 148
  Rothko, Mark, 148
  as a spiritual path, 145
  and surrender to formlessness, described, 145–147, 149, 152, 155
  and Warhol, Andy, 148
ascension, as aroma of infinity, 66–67
ascension, as revelation of the Father
  described, 92–94
  as inhalation of "divine air", 92
  reversal of, 94–97
  See also incarnation; resurrection

attachment, as false identifications, 16, 21, 33–34, 166–167
Avadhuta Gita, 4–5
avadhuta, defined, 48
introduced, 47–48
verses, 48–53
awakening, the act of
compared to dreaming, 169–170
within the context of psychotherapy, 122–130
the thought of enlightenment, 107, 108
awareness
awakening nondual, 123–129
and education, as a mediating force in, 134–135, 140–142
See also awakening; Self-realization
Ayin, 67–68

Bayrack, Shaykh Tosun, al-Jerrahi al-Halveti, 55
Beard, Charles, 123
Be as You Are: The Teachings of Sri Ramana Maharshi (Godman), 11
Beck, Charlotte Joko, 5
"being"
and non-being, 59, 109
and nothingness, 68
perspective of, 190
and Presence, 125
See also Self
Berle, Milton, 137
bhakti, described, 38
blue pill, as symbol of Maya, 168
bodhisattva, 103
bondage, non-existence of, 18–19, 50, 166–167, 171–172
Brahman, 24, 48, 50, 52
See also Absolute, the
Buddhism
Buddha, 190
Eightfold Path of, 116–117
See also Diamond Sutra; *Heart Sutra*

candle and Ein Sof, metaphor of, 66
celebration of nonduality, 184–185
Christ
and ascension, 93–94
death of, 90
as Eternal Form, 89–90, 93–94
and Eucharist, 97
incarnation of, 96–97
the knowing of, 91
as non-separate from the Father, 90, 93
as one's true nature, 90–91
and resurrection, 91
truth of, 96–99
Christianity, as confessed by Bernadette Roberts, 89–99
cinema nondualité, 15, 159–173
consciousness
described by John Wren-Lewis, 6–7
as fashioned by God, 96
limited view of Bernadette Roberts, 89–98

pure view of Ramana Maharshi, 12, 17, 18, 19, 24–25, 38
as *Thuriya*, 170
as truth, 168
See also "being"; Self; truth
Conze, Edward, 108
creativity, as a link to wholeness
art and, 149–150
education and, 132
See also art; education

Dattatreya, life of, 47–48
death
of Christ, 90
metaphoric, especially of artists, 152–153, 157
as truth, 96
deep listening, 157
delusion
of appearances, 108
non-existence of, 18–20
See also ignorance
desire
as manifestation of divine grace, 27–28
for nonduality, 3–7, 12, 46, 187–188, 190
and not swerving, 46
and surrender, 38
and truth, transmission of, 6
destruction of mental tendencies, 16
dhyana [meditation]. *See* meditation
Diamond Sutra
introduced, 101–102
and mind, keeping independence of, 107
and non-attachment, 104
and nothing existing, therefore everything existing, 108–111
and path of the pilgrim, 110
and *Tathagata* (Buddha) having no teaching, 105
understanding of, as greatest merit, 105, 107, 108
See also Heart Sutra
di Grave, Salverda, 56
direct knowledge, red pill as guide to, 167–169
direct path, Self-inquiry as the, 33
Divina Comedia (Dante), 56
"divine air", 92
Christ's body dissolving into, 93–94
and revelation that Christ dwells in the Father, 93
divine state. *See* heaven
dream, the world as a, 108, 169–170
Duchamp, Marcel, 148

Eastman, Charles Alexander (aka Ohiyesa). *See* Ohiyesa
education
and awareness as mediator of information, 134–135, 140–142
and creativity, reorientation toward, 132
and fear, influence of, 140
and information overload, 132–134

education *(continued)*
and questions, value of, 135–140
effort, Self-inquiry and, 20, 27–28
ego
as appearance, 24
as bondage, 19
defined, 12
freedom from idea of, 106
as habitual thoughts, 17
as "I", sense of, 19
as other than Truth, 51
renouncement through surrender, 37, 152
and Self, 19, 21, 24
transcendence of, through Self-inquiry, 23
See also mind; thoughts
Eightfold Path of Buddhism, 116–117
Ein Sof, 64–67
Einstein, Albert, 159
elephants tied to stake, as analogous to mind as prison, 166–167
empathic resonance, and nondual psychotherapy, 128
enlightenment. *See* awakening; *Diamond Sutra*; Self-realization; silence
enquiry. *See* Self-inquiry [*vichara*]
equanimity, 82
Eskimos, 155–156
Eternal Form. *See* Form, Eternal
eternity consciousness, 6
Eucharist, as final word on Christ, 97
existence
doubt regarding, 62
as God, 63–64
and *Heart Sutra*, 184
as nondual, 59–61
of "things" compared to self, 61
as unreal, 17, 18–19, 49
See also "I"-thought (*aham-vritti*); form; Form, Eternal; reality

Fadiman, Dorothy, 158
false identifications, 16, 17, 21, 33–34, 166–167
Father, as the unmanifest, 90, 93–94
fear, 5, 7, 12, 140, 153
Fenner, Peter, 124
form
Heart Sutra and, 181–184
as horizontal dimension of life, 124–125
See also existence; Form, Eternal
Form, Eternal
Christ as, 89–90, 93–94
defined, 89
formlessness
artists' relationship to, 145–147, 149, 152, 154, 155
as confessed in *Avadhuta Gita*, 49, 50, 52
the Father and, 91, 93–94
Heart Sutra and, 181–184
as vertical dimension of life, 125
See also Self
From Deep Woods to Civilization (Eastman), 80

Fukuoka, Masanobu, 181

Gandhi, Mahatma, 167
Gatto, John, 140
God
bringing forth being from nothingness, 68
consciousness fashioned by, 96
existing as one, 37, 63–65, 90–91
grace of, 4–5
making a picture of, 188
in Native American Tradition, 81–83
personal relationship with, 144
surrender to, 36–38
See also Allah; Christ
GOD-AWFULNESS of incarnation, 95–97
Godman, David, 11, 15, 30
grace, 4–5, 12, 27–28
Great Mystery, worship of, 81
Great Silence
in Christianity (Bernadette Roberts), 91
in Native American Tradition, 85
See also silence

Heart, as Self, 20–21, 22, 24, 25
"I-I" shining within the, 36
location of, discussed, 32
See also Self
Heart Sutra
Christian (Bernadette Roberts) expression of, 183–184
Kabbalistic expression of, 182–183
Masanobu Fukuoka expresses, 181
Sufi expression of, 182
Wei Wu Wei expresses, 182
heaven
compared to human condition, 95–97
as destination of artists, 147–148, 151
as not of this world, 93, 96
Herrigel, Eugen, 6
Hixon, Lex, 184–185
Hoffer, Eric, 131
Hui-neng, 163

"I am", as reality, 34–35
"I am not", as reality, 109–110
Ibn 'Arabi, biography of, 55–56
identifications, as false, 16, 17, 21, 33–34, 166–167
ignorance
and *ajnani* (unenlightened person), characteristics of, 21, 24, 25
and false identifications, 16, 17, 21, 33–34, 166–167
and fear, 5, 7, 12, 140, 153
The Matrix as, 172
Maya as, 20
mirror symbolizing, 170–171
as veil over Self, 16–17
See also ego; mind
"I-I", as Self, 36

illusion
 of body-awareness, 168
 casting off of, 36–37
impossible view of nonduality, 7, 189–190
 See also worthwhile view of nonduality
Impressionists, formlessness and the, 147–148
incarnation
 of Christ, 96–97
 described as return to the resurrected state, 94–95
 as GOD-AWFUL, 95–97
 as revelation of truth, 94, 97
 See also ascension, as revelation of the Father; resurrection
inhalation
 of aroma of infinity, 67
 of "divine air", 92–93, 94
 See also ascension, as revelation of the Father
inquiry. *See* Self-inquiry [*vichara*]
Inuit, 155–156
"I"-thought (*aham-vritti*)
 arising in the Heart, 32
 Self-inquiry and following the, 22–23, 26
 true "I" compared to false "I", 33–34
 See also Self-inquiry [*vichara*]

jiva, 17, 22
jnana, 17
jnani, 24
journey
 mythic, of artist, 156
 of Neo, 168
 to resolve desire for nonduality, 7
 revealing truth of Christ, nature of, 98–99
 See also path
Judaism, 63–68

Kabbalah, 63–68
karma [*prarabdha*], 29
Klein, Jean, *29*
knowledge, true, 17–18, 107–108
 See also education; truth

Lao Tzu, on doing our own work first, 156
liberation
 defined, 19
 non-existence of, 18–19, 50
 See also Self-realization
listening, deep, 157
love
 and Ibn 'Arabi, expressed by, 56
 and Native American Tradition, expressed within, 85
 as romantic destiny, in *The Matrix*, 162
 unconditional, 128
 See also Heart, as Self

Mair, Victor H., 69
Many Lightnings, 78
Matrix, The
 and blue pill as Maya, 168

and elephants tied to stake, analogy of, 166–167
illusory nature discussed, 169–170
as Maya, 172
and mind, relationship to, 164–167
mirror symbolizing distortion of thoughts, 170–171
red pill as symbol of guide to direct knowledge, 167–169
spiritual rebirth of Neo described, 173
story summarized, 160–162
unplugging from, 171–172
and the Upanishads as the red pill, 167–169
waking up from, 169–170
See also ego
mauna. *See* silence
Maya, 20
The Matrix as, 172
See also ignorance
meditation
described, 28
obstacles to, 29
and samadhi, compared to, 28
and Self-inquiry, compared to, 34
as true nature, 30
See also Self-inquiry [*vichara*]
metaphors
burning log and function of spiritual teacher, 125–126
candle and *Ein Sof*, 66
elephants tied to stake, 166–167
moon and sun as mind and heart, 21
sparks as ego, 21
See also Matrix, The
mind
destruction of tendencies of the, 16
disappears through Self-inquiry, 25
keeping independence of, 107
and knowing the Self, 20–21, 172
and The Matrix computer, analogous to, 164–165
as obstructing the natural state of peace, 29–30
as prison, 166–167
in reality there is no, 49
See also ego; *Matrix, The*
miracles, 81, 87
mirror
as reflecting truth, 123
as symbolizing ignorance, 170–171
Morpheus. *See Matrix, The*
movies. *See Matrix, The*
Muhammad, Prophet, 58, 59, 61

Nagarjuna, 102
Native American Tradition
and beauty, appreciation of, 86–87
and Great Mystery, worship of, 81
and miracles, 81, 87
and nature as the temple, 81–82

Native American Tradition *(continued)*
and Ohiyesa, biography of, 77–80
and prayer, 84–86
and silence, 82
and simplicity, 83
and solitude, 81, 83
and Spirit of God, 81–83
nature, as a temple, 81–82
Neo. *See Matrix, The*
non-attachment. *See Diamond Sutra*
non-being, and being, 59, 109
nonduality
celebration of, 184–185
described, 3, 4, 12, 122–123, 124
desire for, 3–7, 12, 46, 187–188, 190
impossible view of, 189–190
perspective of, discussed, 115
and psychotherapy, impact on, 124–125
radical descriptions of, 179–180
wisdom and, 5, 122–123
worthwhile view of, 190
See also non-separateness; *various topics in this index*
nondual psychotherapy. *See* psychotherapy, nondual
nonexistence
and Allah, 59
of bondage, 18–19, 50, 166–167, 171–172
of liberation, 18–19, 50
See also formlessness; nothingness
nonexistence, of bondage and liberation, 18–19
See also reality
non-separateness
of art and life, 153–154
of Christ and the Father, 90, 93
and *Diamond Sutra*, 104, 105
of God and you, 37
of Self and mind, 20–21
of a work and the world, 187–188
See also nonduality
no-self condition, 91–92, 95–96
nothing
knowing yourself as, 59, 72, 144
the marketing of, 133–134
nothingness
Heart Sutra expresses, 182–183
Kabbalistic expression of, 66–68
as prior to being, 109
Tao Te Ching expresses, 74
as void of voids, 90

obstacles to Self-realization, 17
Ohiyesa, biography of, 77–80

Palacios, Asin, 56
paradox of Self-realization, 36, 70, 149
path
art as a, 145, 147, 156
as choice between happiness and delusion, 167–168
desire and the, 6–7

direct, 33
Eightfold, 116–117
of the pilgrim, 110
See also journey
peace, attainment of, 29–30
Pinker, Steven, 135
Pollock, Jackson, 148
practices. *See* meditation; prayer; psychotherapy, nondual; Self-inquiry [*vichara*]; surrender
prarabdha [karma], 29
prayer, 84–86
Prendergast, John, J., 121
Presence, role in psychotherapy, 123, 125–126
Price, A.F., 101
psychotherapy, nondual
and acceptance, capacity for, 127–128
and awakening, 129–130
codification of, concerns with, 124
Eastern influence on, 121–122
and empathic resonance, 128
and nonduality itself, impact of, 124–125
and Presence, role of, 123, 125–126
and sacred mirroring, as reflecting essential nature, 123
and self-identity of the psychotherapist, 126–128
and Self-inquiry, 128–129
and truth, transmission of, 126
See also Self-inquiry [*vichara*]
questions, value in education, 135–140

Ramakrishna, 147
Ramana Maharshi, introduced, 11–13
See also Self; Self-inquiry [*vichara*]; Self-realization
reality
nature of, 50–51, 169–170
and non-reality, 109–110
See also existence; *Matrix, The*
red pill, as symbol of guide to direct knowledge, 167–169
resurrection
as affirming ultimate truth, 91
and ascension, compared to, 93
described, 90–91
and Eucharistic state, 97
incarnation and, 94–95
and no-self condition, acclimating to, 91–92, 95–96
and "smile of recognition", 90, 91
See also ascension, as revelation of the Father; incarnation
Rothko, Mark, 148
Rumi, *23*

sacred mirroring, as reflecting truth, 123
samadhi
compared to meditation, 28
existence of, questioned, 51
scriptures, red pill as, 167–169
See also topics from major religions

sefirot, 66, 67
Self
  abidance in the, 17–18, 28
  defined, 11
  and ego, 19, 21
  and false identifications, 16, 17, 21, 33–34, 166–167
  as Heart, 20–21, 22, 24, 25
  as "I-I", 36
  and mind, 20–21
  no reaching the, 16
  not swerving from the, 28
  as one's truth, 61
  searching for the, 26
  Thuriya as the, 170
  and unplugging from Maya, 172
  See also Self-inquiry [*vichara*]; Self-realization
Self-inquiry [*vichara*]
  as all the aspirant has to know, 25–26
  and being "I am", 34–35
  compared to meditation, 34
  and conduct in life, 29
  as direct path, 33
  and effort, 20, 27–28
  as following the "I"-thought, 22–23
  and grace, 27–28
  introduced, 18–19
  as not intellectual, 28
  practice of, 29
  and psychotherapy, use in, 128–129
  pursuing in the Heart, 32
  questioning, "Who am I?", 36
  red pill as, 168–169
  and Self-realization, same as, 34
  as turning toward the Heart, 20–21
  See also Self; Self-realization
Self-realization
  described, 16
  as destruction of Maya, 20
  obstacles to, 17
  paradox of, 36
  as perfect effort, 20
  as possible for everyone, 17, 19
  and Self-inquiry, same as, 34
  See also Self; Self-inquiry [*vichara*]
Shankar, Vijay, 169–170
silence
  as death, 91
  as egoless, 38
  as nondual state, 37
  as perfect effort, 20
  as shining in the Heart, 36
  as sign of perfect equilibrium, 82
  surrender to, 129
  as true state, 19
Silence, Great. *See* Great Silence
simplicity
  artist staying in touch with, 155
  of *Ayin*, 67
  in Native American Tradition, 83
  "of the unhewn log", 75
Sioux tradition. *See* Native American Tradition
"smile of recognition", 90, 91, 190

Socrates, and value of questions, 137–140
solitude, 81, 83
sorrow/delusion, non-existence of, 18–19
Spirit of God, 81–83
spiritual path. *See* path
Subhuti. *See Diamond Sutra*
suffering
  questioned, 50
  and right view, 116
Sufism. *See* Allah
surrender
  avoidance of, 152–153
  as beyond death, 152
  and desire, 38
  discussed by Ramana Maharshi, 36–38
  and ego destruction, 37
  to formlessness, 145–147, 149, 152, 155
  and God as not separate from you, 37
  and Self-inquiry, relation to, 37
  to silence, 129

Taoism. *See Tao Te Ching*
Tao Te Ching
  and eternal Way, 73
  on integrity and the Way, 71–72
  on nonaction, 72
  on nothingness, usefulness of, 74
  popularity of, reasons for, 69–70
  on sages, as self-effacing, 72–73
  on simplicity, 75
  verses from, 71–75
Tathagata (Buddha). *See Diamond Sutra*
thoughts
  annihilation of, 68
  and brain biochemistry, 165–166
  disruption of, 168–169
  identity based on, 164–165
  rejection of, 27
  as Sentinels in *Matrix Revolutions*, 165–166
  See also "I"-thought (*aham-vritti*); mind
Thuriya, as Self, 170
Tirumoolar, 172, 173
Tolle, Eckhart, 125–126
Trinity. *See Matrix, The*
true knowledge, described, 17
truth
  abidance in, 108
  of the body, 91
  of Christ, 96–99
  as death of man, 97
  and desire, 6
  and disruption of thoughts, 168–169
  as eternity consciousness, 6–7
  and grace, 5
  incarnation as revelation of, 94, 97
  living by, 6
  The Matrix prevents one from knowing the, 163–164
  nondual characteristics of, described, 4, 50–52

truth *(continued)*
psychotherapy as transmitter of, 126
resurrection affirming, 91
sacred mirror reflecting, 123
struggle to recognize, 171–173
that is right before you, 189
See also Absolute, the; Self; Self-realization

Upadesa Manjari (Venkatasubramanian and Godman), 30
Upanishads, red pill as, 167–169

vasanas, destruction of, 16
Venkataraman, 12–13
Venkatasubramanian, V.T., 30
vichara [inquiry]. *See* Self-inquiry [*vichara*]
Vivekananda, Swami, 48
void
the artist leaping into the, 144, 158
and Eternal Form, relation to, 89–90
and Heart Sutra, 182
of voids, Christ as, 90–91
See also formlessness

Wabasha, 82
waking. *See* awakening
Warhol, Andy, 148
Way, the
integrity and, 70, 71–72
of the Spirit, 81–87
Wei Wu Wei, 108
wholeness
and art, as the spirit of, 151
and education, as the spirit of, 132
"Why?", as question driving creativity, 135–137
Wilber, Ken, 123
wisdom, nonduality and, 5, 122–123
Wizard of Oz, The, 4
worship, of Great Mystery, 81
worthwhile view of nonduality, 7, 190
See also impossible view of nonduality
Wren-Lewis, John, 6–7

Zen in the Art of Archery (Herrigel), 6

About the Editor

JERRY KATZ received an M.S. in biology from the University of New Mexico. He has been interested in human consciousness since childhood, and has investigated many spiritual teachings. In 1997, he introduced the website that would become Nonduality.com, which brings the teaching of nonduality to an audience beyond ashrams and academic institutions. In 1998, he founded Nonduality Salon, an email forum that recognizes and welcomes both the "impossible" and the "worthwhile" expressions of nonduality. Since 1998, Jerry has published a free daily email letter, *The Nondual Highlights.* He lives in Halifax, Nova Scotia.

For more information, please see www.nonduality.com.

Sentient Publications, LLC publishes books on cultural creativity, experimental education, transformative spirituality, holistic health, new science, ecology, and other topics, approached from an integral viewpoint. Our authors are intensely interested in exploring the nature of life from fresh perspectives, addressing life's great questions, and fostering the full expression of the human potential. Sentient Publications' books arise from the spirit of inquiry and the richness of the inherent dialogue between writer and reader.

We are very interested in hearing from our readers. To direct suggestions or comments to us, or to be added to our mailing list, please contact:

SENTIENT PUBLICATIONS, LLC
1113 Spruce Street
Boulder, CO 80302
303-443-2188
contact@sentientpublications.com
www.sentientpublications.com